WHAT YOUR COLLEAGUES ARE SAYING ...

"*Daily Routines to Jump-Start Math Class* provides easily implemented, highly engaging activities for students to develop fluency and flexibility with number operations, foster reasoning, and further develop number sense. This book is a game changer for teachers to have easily implemented routines that not only provide rich formative data about content and mathematical practices but also replace the mundane activities typically utilized at the opening of a math class."

Natalie Crist
Supervisor of Elementary Mathematics
Baltimore County Public Schools
Baltimore, MD

"These routines have revolutionized our daily instruction—our students *beg* to do number routines every day! Straightforward and easy to implement with little or no prep, these routines change students' thinking about math in a positive way. Our students are more engaged and students at all ages are building better number sense."

Marissa Walsh
Elementary Math Coach
Blue Springs School District
Blue Springs, MO

"Classroom teachers will be jumping with excitement when they discover John SanGiovanni's *Daily Routines to Jump-Start Math Class*. This long-awaited elementary book is ready for immediate use and offers high-quality thinking and reasoning number routines teachers want and need to use with students. Teachers will find this book to be the perfect tool for practicing critical skills and concepts and will absolutely love choosing daily routines that make a difference."

Ruth Harbin Miles
Mary Baldwin University
Staunton, VA

"What a helpful resource! *Daily Routines to Jump-Start Math Class* does just that and so much more! These routines and their many extensions truly engage students in developing and extending their sense of number while emphasizing the importance of reasoning."

Francis (Skip) Fennell
Director, Elementary Mathematics Specialists and Teacher Leaders Project
Professor of Education and Graduate and Professional Studies, Emeritus
McDaniel College
Westminster, MD

"If you are an elementary teacher who is looking for math tasks that are easy to implement, build number sense, and encourage collaboration among students this resource is for you! *Daily Routines to Jump-Start Math Class* provides engaging tasks that will get your students thinking and reasoning about mathematics within the first minute of your math lesson. John SanGiovanni provides all of the support you will need to get these quick, easy-to-prepare routines implemented in your own classroom."

Susie Katt
K–2 Mathematics Coordinator
Lincoln Public Schools
Lincoln, NE

"Designing and implementing regular opportunities for students to develop, use, and apply number sense is the hallmark of effective teaching. In *Daily Routines to Jump-Start Math Class: Engage Students, Improve Number Sense, and Practice Reasoning,* author John SanGiovanni provides an incredible variety of number sense routines that will engage students in reasoning about mathematics in positive and productive ways. With 20 unique routines at their fingertips, teachers can mindfully and purposefully engage students in mathematics discourse that will bolster students' learning strengths and needs."

Beth Kobett
Board of Directors, National Council of the Teachers of Mathematics
Associate Professor, School of Education
Stevenson University
Stevenson, MD

"This is a fantastic collection of engaging and meaningful routines, a must-own for K–5 teachers. For teachers, the instructions are straightforward and the examples very helpful. For students, these are fun and challenging! For both, there are so many great routines, that won't get old, and the routines address a great mix of mathematics (whole numbers, fractions, operations, geometry, etc.) and learning tools (number lines, pictures, graphic organizers, etc.). Estimation, such a difficult and important topic, is effectively addressed in numerous routines! I will be sharing the ideas from this book with teachers at all levels—elementary mathematics specialists and preservice teachers—helping them to see how many ways they can engage students in mathematical reasoning and sense making!"

Jennifer M. Bay-Williams
Mathematics Educator and Professor
University of Louisville
Louisville, KY

Daily Routines to Jump-Start Math Class, Elementary
THE BOOK AT-A-GLANCE

A quick-reference table provides you with a brief description of each task, along with the corresponding task purpose.

JUMP-START ROUTINES AT-A-GLANCE

	ROUTINE	DESCRIPTION	PURPOSE
1	Math Yapper	Students provide clues for partners to guess mystery numbers, concepts, or vocabulary.	Develop understanding of concepts and vocabulary to communicate clearly.
2	The Count	Students make predictions about counting when given starting points and an interval.	Develop counting and skip-counting skills and estimation.
3	The Missing	Students determine missing numbers on a number chart.	Develop advanced strategies about counting.
4	Big or Small	Students determine when a number represents something big and when a number represents something small.	Develop sense of quantity and magnitude through contexts for number.
5	Picture It	Students estimate quantities in pictures.	Develop understanding of magnitude of numbers by reasoning about them in context.
6	Show It 3	Students represent a number in three diverse ways.	Develop deeper understanding of single and multi-digit number concepts.
7	How Can You Make It?	Students determine ways to make a number.	Develop understanding of number composition and decomposition.
8	The Mighty Ten	Students find combinations of 10, multiples of 10, 100, or 1,000.	Develop fluency with combinations of ten and transfer this fluency to multi-digit numbers.
9	Make It Friendly	Students add more than one number by finding friendly numbers.	Develop strategies for adding and subtracting numbers using decomposition and compatible numbers.
10	Mystery Number	Students use clues about a number to determine if they have the mystery number.	Develop understanding about number through attributes and relationships.
11	Number Bio	Students complete prompts about a given number.	Develop understanding about numbers through representations, attributes, and relationships.
12	Condition	Students use conditions about a number to earn points.	Develop understanding of number and flexibility of reasoning.
13	Where's the Point?	Students determine possible values for unknown locations on empty number lines.	Develop understanding of number relationships with number lines.

Video Demonstrations bring the jump-start routines to life and help you visualize how they might work in your classroom.

PART 2

JUMP-START ROUTINES

VIDEO DEMONSTRATIONS:

 The Count

 Where's the Point?

 The Missing

 Is This the End?

 Big or Small

 More or Less

 Show It 3

 This or That?

 How Can You Make It?

 Another Way to Say It

 Condition

 The Truth

 All videos can be viewed at resources.corwin.com/jumpstartroutines/elementary

An **About the Routine** section provides an overview of what the routine entails.

THE MISSING (COUNTING AND SKIP-COUNTING)

● About the Routine

Students learn about and use all sorts of tools to help them count and make sense of number relationships. A number chart is one of the most fundamental tools that students work with. Though this tool is instrumental, if not used well, it can undermine student progress toward more complex ideas about numbers and counting. Often, missing numbers on the chart are surrounded by known or completed numbers. In some cases, the entire chart is completed with the exception of a handful of *missing* numbers. Students are then asked to find the missing numbers. Students are likely to simply count on from knowns. Unfortunately, some students may still begin with 1 and count on to find the missing number, even though many of the numbers are already present. There are missed opportunities to discuss other counting strategies, including 10 more and 10 less, two more and two less, and so on. *The Missing* asks students to find

1	2	3	4	5	6	7	8		
							17		
31									
			54						
61									
								80	
								90	
			95						

specific missing numbers with few markers to offer support. After finding targeted unknowns, students then share how they counted thus exposing others to possibly unknown, unfamiliar, or uncomfortable counting strategies.

● Why It Matters

This routine helps students:

- persevere when solutions or solution paths are not obvious (MP1);
- reinforce relationships between numbers (MP2);
- discover that numbers are related to other numbers in more than one way (MP2);
- look for patterns within counting numbers, known and unknown numbers (MP7);

- make use of structure when counting (MP8);
- better understand how number charts work and support thinking (MP5); and
- communicate their strategies to others (MP3).

> online resources
> All tasks can be downloaded for your use at **resources.corwin.com/ jumpstartroutines/elementary**

Why It Matters sections encapsulate the relevance of the routine for student learning and call out any related Standards for Mathematical Practice.

Online Resources icons signal the availability of downloadable tasks.

What They Should Understand First sections explain what mathematics students should ideally know before embarking on the routine at hand.

What to Do sections break down exactly how to use the routine in your classroom, step by step.

What They Should Understand First

How Do You Make It? works with any number or type of number, including fractions and decimals. You should use it after students show conceptual understanding of number and decomposition. They might show understanding through a collection of representations, but they must also be able to communicate how those representations connect to symbolic representations (numbers). Students should also show some ability to decompose a number. In kindergarten, decomposition might be limited to *one-more than* or *two-more than* a number. For example, they might only be able to think of 11 as 1 and 10 or 2 and 9. In later grades, decomposition might be limited to place value. Either is fine. The routine itself is intended to expose, develop, and reinforce new ideas about decomposing numbers. You might provide students with tools, such as 10 frames or base 10 blocks, during initial exposures to the routine. In these early experiences, you should also record and connect symbolic decompositions to representations if students do not do so themselves.

What to Do

1. Select a number for students to decompose. (Note: Consider giving some examples of how it might be decomposed the first few times the routine is introduced.)

2. Direct students to decompose the number. (Optional: Have students decompose the number in two ways or more than three ways.)

3. Have students share their decomposition(s) with a partner.

4. Have students share their examples with the group.

5. Record student examples. Note that there is no better number of examples to record. In some instances, five will be plenty. In others, nine or 10 examples might be collected and recorded.

6. Discuss with the group the decomposition examples that were recorded. Questions to ask might include:

   » What do you notice about how we decomposed the number?

   » What two decompositions are most alike?

   » How did the numbers in those examples change?

   » Do you notice any patterns in how we broke apart the numbers?

   » Do you think this pattern will work with other numbers?

   » Which of the examples are easiest for you to think about?

   » Which of the examples are hardest for you to think about?

7. After discussion, ask students to decompose the number in a new way that wasn't recorded.

8. Have students share their new decompositions with partners and then the whole class.

Anticipated Strategies for This Example

How can you make **15**?

For this example, students are asked to decompose 15. It is a good choice for later in the kindergarten year or early in first grade. Many students are likely to first decompose 15 into 10 and 5. Some students may be able to only decompose it into 10 and 5. Students who extend beyond place value decomposition are likely to use breaking a number into 1 and something and 2 and something. In this example, that would be 14 and 1 and 13 and 2. You should listen for students who consistently share something and 1 or something and 2 for different reasons. Some who rely on a number and 1 (14 and 1) might think of it in ways of counting and may not recognize that it is a decomposition. Those that understand might

Anticipated Strategies for This Example describe and distill the key strategies that will likely arise while students are working through each routine.

Additional Examples sections explain how you can adjust the routine for grade-specific content and leverage it to further develop students' mathematical skills.

They might avoid three-digit numbers with the same digit in each place value. As you notice these vacancies in student creations, you can pose new conditions to *nudge* your students toward thinking about *different* numbers. For example, you may find that no student numbers have a 0 in them. The next condition you pose could award a point for a number that has zero tens. And, you might ask it again the next day to get a sense if any students latched on to the thought that a three-digit number can have zero tens. Some conditions in the routine are better suited for reasoning and discussion than others. The third condition in the featured example petitions for numbers that round to 700. Some students will think of numbers between 650 and 699, others will think of numbers between 700 and 749, and others will identify both sets. This is an example of a condition prompt that has potential for rich discussion.

CONDITION—ADDITIONAL EXAMPLES

A. You can use *Condition* with all elementary students, as you can easily modify it for any concept or range of numbers. Example A shows how you might use it in a kindergarten classroom. The two 10 frames captured in the image are available with the slide deck in the downloadable content. You could also choose to have a large double 10 frame on the board that can be manipulated. For young students, you might choose to have them make a model of their number before posing conditions. Conditions themselves can make use of representations. You

A

Create a number on your ten frames.
Match the **CONDITION** to earn a point.

Your number
- is the smallest number in the class
- is more than 10
- is one more than 7
- is more than 12
- is two more than 4

IS THIS THE END? VARIATION—DIFFERENT KNOWNS

One location was given in the previous examples. You can take another approach to the routine as well. You could ask students to find locations other than endpoints. Or, you might provide an endpoint and a known location and ask students to place other numbers on the number line.

E. Clearly, Example E is quite different than the other examples of the routine. But, the thinking and reasoning remains the same. Students still have to think about how numbers are related to one another. In fact, it still makes use of a midpoint. As noted in the directions, it is fine for you to tell students that the arrow/value is exactly in the middle of the number line. In this example, knowing that the middle is 20 other relationships have to be considered. What would the right endpoint be? Are all of the options presented (10, 22, and 45) possibilities for this number line as drawn? 45 isn't on this number line as drawn. It would be just past the right endpoint. It would also be acceptable for students to extend the number line to justify where 45 should be placed.

E

The arrow is pointing at 20.
About where is 10? 22? 45?

0

F. A criticism of number line use is that the endpoints are often stagnant and rely on a left endpoint of 0. This is not to say those endpoints

F

Variations on each routine are provided to further deepen student understanding and provide ways to meet the varied needs of your learners.

DAILY ROUTINES to JUMP-START MATH CLASS

ELEMENTARY SCHOOL

DAILY ROUTINES to JUMP-START MATH CLASS

ELEMENTARY SCHOOL

Engage Students, Improve Number Sense, and Practice Reasoning

JOHN J.
SANGIOVANNI

CORWIN Mathematics

FOR INFORMATION:

Corwin

A SAGE Company

2455 Teller Road

Thousand Oaks, California 91320

(800) 233–9936

www.corwin.com

SAGE Publications Ltd.

1 Oliver's Yard

55 City Road

London, EC1Y 1SP

United Kingdom

SAGE Publications India Pvt. Ltd.

B 1/I 1 Mohan Cooperative Industrial Area

Mathura Road, New Delhi 110 044

India

SAGE Publications Asia-Pacific Pte. Ltd.

18 Cross Street #10–10/11/12

China Square Central

Singapore 048423

Printed in the United States of America.

Library of Congress Cataloging-in-Publication Data

Names: SanGiovanni, John, author.

Title: Daily routines to jump-start math class, elementary : engage students, improve number sense, and practice reasoning / John J. SanGiovanni.

Description: Thousand Oaks, California : Corwin, [2020] | Includes bibliographical references.

Identifiers: LCCN 2019012499 | ISBN 9781544374949 (pbk. : alk. paper)

Subjects: LCSH: Mathematics teachers–In-service training. | Mathematics–Study and teaching (Elementary) | Elementary school teachers–In-service training.

Classification: LCC QA10.5 .S26 2020 | DDC 372.7–dc23 LC record available at https://lccn.loc.gov/2019012499

This book is printed on acid-free paper.

Executive Editor, Mathematics: Erin Null

Associate Content
    Development Editor: Jessica Vidal

Production Editor: Tori Mirsadjadi

Copy Editor: Laurie Pitman

Typesetter: Integra

Proofreader: Susan Schon

Cover and Interior Designer: Scott Van Atta

Marketing Manager: Margaret O'Connor

Certified Chain of Custody
Promoting Sustainable Forestry
www.sfiprogram.org
SFI-01268

SFI label applies to text stock

19 20 21 22 23 10 9 8 7 6 5 4 3 2 1

CONTENTS

Acknowledgments   xv

About the Author   xvii

PART I: WHY JUMP-START ROUTINES?   1

The First Few Minutes of Mathematics Class   1

Opportunities for Better Engagement and High-Quality Practice   4

Jump-Start Routines: New Warm-ups for a New Era   5

Implementing Jump-Start Routines   10

Plan for the Routine   12

Practical Advice for Routines   17

PART II: JUMP-START ROUTINES   21

Routine 1: Math Yapper   22

Routine 2: The Count   29

Routine 3: The Missing   36

Routine 4: Big or Small   42

Routine 5: Picture It   48

Routine 6: Show It 3   55

Routine 7: How Can You Make It?   62

Routine 8: The Mighty Ten   69

Routine 9: Make It Friendly   76

Routine 10: Mystery Number   83

Routine 11: Number Bio   90

Routine 12: Condition   96

Routine 13: Where's the Point?   102

Routine 14: Is This the End?   109

Routine 15: About or Between   116

Routine 16: More or Less   123

Routine 17: This or That?   130

Routine 18: Finding One and All   137

Routine 19: Another Way to Say It   144

Routine 20: The Truth   151

PART III: WHERE TO GO NEXT   **157**

Make a Plan   **157**

Adjust to Their Adjustments   **159**

Further Modify Routines   **159**

Design Your Own Routines   **160**

Work Collaboratively and Share the Load   **160**

Use Jump-Start Routines for Professional Learning or PLCs   **161**

Jump-Start Mathematics Engagement, Number Sense, and Reasoning   **162**

Appendix   **163**

References   **164**

 Visit the companion website at **http://resources.corwin.com/ jumpstartroutines/elementary** for downloadable resources.

Note From the Publisher: Video and web content throughout the book is available to you through QR (quick response) codes. To read a QR code, you must have a smartphone or tablet with a camera. We recommend that you download a QR code reader app that is made specifically for your phone or tablet brand.

Videos may also be accessed at **resources.corwin.com/jumpstartroutines/elementary**

ACKNOWLEDGMENTS

This book has been a collaborative effort. I am grateful to Corwin for making it a reality. I am thankful that they recognize the importance of reasoning, number sense, computational fluency, discussion, and student engagement. I appreciate that they, too, know that we can develop these in our students through engaging activities that are practical and doable.

I am incredibly grateful for my district mathematics team. They are leaders in every sense of the word. They strive for better mathematics for each and every student. They are creative, dedicated, and usually fun to work with. I must acknowledge Heather Dyer as her work and vision made routines the cornerstone of our mathematics program. Our mathematics coaches have also played a critical role in filming early versions of our take on number routines. They have spent countless hours supporting teachers so that their students could have number sense and reasoning opportunities that many of us didn't have.

The work of so many of us is possible because of the greatness that *paved the way* for us. Skip Fennell, Barbara Reys, Robert Reys, Leigh Childs, Laura Chote, and so many more have helped me see so many *cool* ways to play with numbers and engage students. Their ideas inspire new twists, new applications, new books, and new blog posts. I would be remiss if I didn't give a special thanks to Skip. Words cannot say enough. So, I'll simply buy the next round or two. Thanks to my many other math friends who make me better. And as always, thanks to Kay Sammons. She took a chance a long time ago on a young guy who didn't know much.

I would like to especially thank the following teachers, coaches, and administrators who embody the best of mathematics education. They welcomed me into their school classrooms to record these jump-start routines in action. These brief videos bring the activities to life and help readers better understand how to implement them in their classrooms. Those individuals are Summer Appler, Megan Jefferson, Emily Nupp, Emily O'Connor, Lauren Pate, Kristen Mangus, and Troy Todd.

Thanks to the staff at Corwin for transforming a featureless document file into such an appealing, practical tool for teaching and learning. Special thanks to Erin Null (again) for her enthusiasm, partnership, thoughtful questions, insight, and friendship.

Lastly and most importantly, many thanks to my family. I can never thank them enough.

PUBLISHER'S ACKNOWLEDGMENTS

Corwin gratefully acknowledges the contributions of the following reviewers:

Francis (Skip) Fennell
Director, Elementary Mathematics Specialists
    and Teacher Leaders Project
Professor of Education and Graduate and
    Professional Studies, Emeritus
McDaniel College, Westminster, MD

Susie Katt
K–2 Mathematics Coordinator
Lincoln Public Schools
Lincoln, NE

Monica Tienda
Elementary Teacher
Oak Park School District
Oak Park, MI

ABOUT THE AUTHOR

 **John J. SanGiovanni** is a mathematics supervisor in Howard County, Maryland. There, he leads mathematics curriculum development, digital learning, assessment, and professional development for 42 elementary schools and more than 1,500 teachers. John is an adjunct professor and coordinator of the Elementary Mathematics Instructional Leader graduate program at McDaniel College. He is an author and national mathematics curriculum and professional learning consultant. John is a frequent speaker at national conferences and institutes. He is active in state and national professional organizations recently serving on the Board of Directors for the National Council of Teachers of Mathematics and currently as the president of the Maryland Council of Supervisors of Mathematics.

WHY JUMP-START ROUTINES?

THE FIRST FEW MINUTES OF MATHEMATICS CLASS

The start of an elementary mathematics class varies greatly from classroom to classroom, grade to grade, and school to school. It might be a mad rush to get our students settled as they come into the room in the morning, from recess, or from related arts. It might be a blurred start as we change topics from science or social studies to mathematics. It might be the first few minutes of our instructional day, or it might be the last hour of our day. Regardless of how or when it begins, the first few minutes of our mathematics class has the potential to shape the entire lesson by setting tone and purpose.

The first few minutes are an opportunity for us to capture the attention of our students and prepare them for the lesson ahead. These opening minutes are also the time when our students' brains are freshest. They tend to remember more of what we teach or do during this segment than any other time of the learning episode (Sousa, 2007). That is why it is such a critical time for us to help students shed their distractions, capture their attention, and jump-start their brains. Engaging students immediately will increase the likelihood that they'll stay engaged and motivated to learn throughout the lesson.

However, we don't always take advantage of those precious first few minutes. We have felt obligated to meet the long-held traditions about how mathematics class *must* begin. We have come to find that the activities instead undermine our goals and the productive beliefs we have about teaching and learning mathematics. First and foremost, we have all experienced our instructional time being hijacked by opening calendar rituals, traditional warm-ups, and homework review. It is difficult to keep each of these from going beyond the allotted time. We have had them unravel, becoming unwanted mini-lessons disconnected from the intended objective because we want to help our students. These opening activities also often focus on the goal of getting right answers. They cause us to begin class by setting the tone that mathematics is the pursuit of answers.

Ineffective Calendar Rituals

Calendar rituals are daily ceremonies made up of a series of actions carried out in a specific order. Often, students complete patterns, graph observations about weather, and categorize numbers in a variety of ways. The intent is to revisit certain mathematics concepts over and over again so that they are understood well. But, we find that these calendar rituals quickly become mindless actions. Our students' engagement quickly wanes. Their thinking and reasoning fall behind process and procedure as they complete the tasks mechanically. Mathematics becomes an experience grounded in compliance and completion rather than being rich and dynamic. But, what if it didn't?

Traditional Warm-ups

Unfortunately, the first five minutes of most classes are often spent on logistical or low-level cognitive tasks such as taking attendance, reviewing homework, or completing problems that are identical to homework problems assigned the night before. While the goal may be to tap into prior learning, such problems are usually rote in nature and ask students to perform simple tasks that often stress procedure and *correctness*. A traditional 3rd grade warm-up might look like this:

Figure 1.1

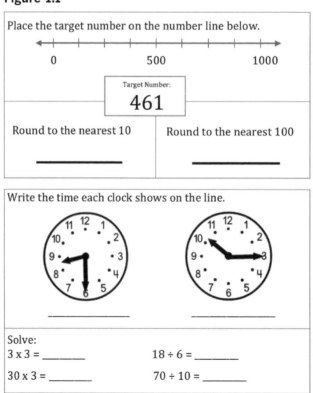

Positioning warm-ups like these as the first *instructional* tasks presents challenges. It signals to students that mathematics is the pursuit of low-level answers and procedures. It suggests that mathematics is a collection of semi-connected ideas and steps. Students may infer that you value these sorts of problems more than others. Why else would you start with them? These problems tell your students that you need them to consistently review ideas because you aren't confident or convinced that they have mastered the skills within them. These warm-ups may fail to take advantage of the moments in which your students' brains are most ready to learn. The most problematic aspect of these warm-ups may be that they fail to set the stage for engagement and discussion.

We know from experience that great lessons begin with a strong start. Many, if not all, of us would agree that the opening minutes of class have the potential to ignite engagement and take advantage of our students' brains being ready to learn. Conversely, a start to class that drags or is uninteresting can sabotage the rest of the period. The traditional warm-up often sets the stage for the latter. But, what if it didn't?

The Problem With Going Over Homework

The effect of homework is muddied. Practice does contribute to achievement. But, who is practicing when elementary homework is completed? Are students completing the homework independently? Do all students have the same resources at home? Is traditional, worksheet-based homework good for young students in general?

Cooper notes that some suggest a link between homework and achievement (Cooper, 2006). However, he also notes that "these results suggest little or no relationship between homework and achievement for elementary school students." According to two studies of middle school and high school mathematics classrooms, 15 to 20 percent of class time tends to be spent reviewing homework (Grouws, Tarr, Sears, & Ross, 2010; Otten, Herbel-Eisenmann, & Cirillo, 2012). One could argue that elementary classrooms see a similar rate. This book is written with the fundamental belief that reviewing homework for any significant time of class is an ineffective way to begin class.

Reviewing homework is another unwritten obligation for planning mathematics class. For a long time, it was thought of as how math should start or something that should be done right after a warm-up. But, it is not a requirement for effective mathematics instruction (NCTM, 2014). In fact, it can contribute to the opposite of effective mathematics instruction. So why is going over homework problematic?

- Certain items within an assignment may be poorly written or uniquely complicated. Time and effort spent to help students *fix it* is wasted.

- Homework should be practice of mastered skills and concepts. If those skills aren't well understood, an ad-hoc mini-lesson comes about diverting instructional time for the intentionally planned lesson.

- Students might not complete homework independently. Time spent in class to go over work completed with parents is counterintuitive. These students may have no better understanding than their classmates but their *work* shows otherwise.

- Some students don't have access to resources at home to complete their homework so there is nothing to go over. Incompleteness of homework means that class time dedicated to reviewing it is already compromised.

The bottom line is we can use brief homework assignments appropriately to reinforce existing knowledge and keep student skills fresh. In doing so, we shouldn't need much, if any, class time to go over it. Instead, we can use that time more productively. We can take back the time lost to rote warm-ups and homework review by starting math class with number sense and reasoning routines. We can engage students and foster their curiosity and creative thinking at the immediate start of class.

OPPORTUNITIES FOR BETTER ENGAGEMENT AND HIGH-QUALITY PRACTICE

Jump-start routines may be best used to help you take back the power of the first few minutes of mathematics class. But, these routines can naturally complement other parts of your class as well. They can help you think about alternatives to other challenges you face. Those challenges include the large collection of practice sheets and busywork provided by your textbook programs. You might swap out some games and centers that don't fulfill your intentions with number sense routines. You might be looking for better ways to help your students realize fluency. Or, you might simply need to build a larger collection of engaging activities because you don't have enough. You might worry that adding in jump-start routines is just another thing to do in an already crowded lesson. But, the below outlines some activities you might consider replacing, making room for these opportunities for better engagement and high-quality practice.

Replacing Busy Work and Drill and Kill

Concerns about mathematics class are not relegated to the first minutes of class. The amount of time we lost to busy work is equally problematic. Practice of skills and concepts is needed. But, practice has the potential to become nothing more than a *time filler*. Our experiences as students as well as the mathematics programs we use frame practice as student workbooks or worksheets. These activities embody all that is meant by *drill and kill*. If we overuse these, our students might begin to see practice and even the purpose of mathematics as compliance and completion. These practices may kill the joy of mathematics causing many students to fall out of love with math.

A greater hazard for most, if not all, of these practice sheets is that they focus on narrow, procedural approaches to mathematics. They don't allow for much critical thinking or reasoning. Discussion is unnecessary, and if it does occur, it is about how something was completed rather than why. There isn't much to think or talk about when the prompts are basic facts, telling time, or rounding such as shown in Figure 1.1 on page 2. Instead, jump-start routines can take the place of some of the more traditional openers in ways that benefit students more than homework review or practice sheets. These routines might also do well to limit, if not supplant, mundane practice as well.

As Alternatives to Games and Centers

Games and centers can be a good way to practice mathematics. Games engage students. They develop strategic thinking and reasoning. But without accountability, students end up being semi-engaged with games talking about random things between lackadaisical engagement. Games can be challenging and undesirable for students who aren't competitive. Like games, centers provide opportunities for worthwhile practice but can be problematic when accountability and feedback are lacking. To be clear, games and centers are good for our students. But, we can complement their use with other engaging practices that offer more accountability, richer discussions, and better feedback. These routines are those worthy complements.

As Different Approaches to Fluency

Students who are fluent are efficient, flexible, and accurate (National Research Council, 2001). Fluency extends beyond basic facts. Students can become fluent with multi-digit computation, fraction comparison, estimation, procedure, and a host of other skills and concepts. As we know, traditional approaches to fact fluency, including games and flash card practice, come up short. Often, these activities don't enable the rich discussions we strive for in our mathematics classes. But, it is difficult for us to find worthy replacements for these activities. Jump-start routines can help solve this problem.

As Part of a Robust, Diverse Collection of Engagement Resources

Number Talks (Parrish, 2010) and online routines such as Which One Doesn't Belong (Wyborney, 2018) and Splat (Wyborney, 2018) are also great choices for filling the fluency practice void. These routines help develop computational fluency, reasoning, and decomposition. But, there is so much more we want our students to practice. And, it can be challenging to maintain our students' interest and engagement if these are our only options over 180 days of mathematics instruction. We need a robust collection of activities that are similarly interesting. We need other activities for other important ideas like counting, magnitude, and estimation. Jump-start routines are the perfect complement.

JUMP-START ROUTINES: NEW WARM-UPS FOR A NEW ERA

The routines in this book are designed to *jump-start* mathematics class. They are new warm-ups for a new era. They are the perfect tool for practicing critical skills and concepts. They are engaging opportunities for students to work with and discuss interesting prompts. The routines are designed to develop students' reasoning and/or sense making. They aim at improving students' number sense. They are a makeover for the beginning and traditional practice activities so that students have access to meaningful, engaging, quality practice. These routines can repair or instill mathematics confidence in our students.

These routines are:

- practical and easy for you to implement each day;
- meant for the first five to seven minutes of class;
- flexible for use in place of other practice activities;
- thinking exercises meant to ignite thinking and reasoning skills;
- open and flexible in nature; and
- modifiable to work with almost any content at any grade level.

These routines create an environment in which the Common Core State Standards for Mathematics (National Governors Association Center for Best Practices & Council of Chief State School Officers, 2010) come to life. Though specific practices are linked to each routine throughout the book (listed as **MP**), in general students will:

1. make sense of problems and persevere;
2. reason abstractly and quantitatively;
3. construct viable arguments and critique the reasoning of others;
4. model with mathematics;
5. use appropriate tools strategically;
6. attend to precision;
7. look for and make use of structure; and
8. look for and express regularity in repeated reasoning.

What Is Meant by Routine?

A routine is an activity that is done, well, routinely. It has a definitive shape and structure. It offers a consistent process so that students can focus on substance rather than sequence steps. Routines become a habit that maximize opportunity. You can easily adjust and customize a routine for any classroom or grade level. There are a wide variety of routines for instruction. There are routines in language arts for phonics and fluency. There are routines for behavior management. There are even other routines in mathematics, including routines for solving problems, reasoning, and discussion. The number routines presented here are for reasoning and number sense.

What Is a Number Routine?

The number routines presented here are structures for talking about numbers, number concepts, and number sense. These routines afford students opportunity to play with numbers. They are flexible yet intentional. They target specific components of number sense. These routines intend to engage students in discussion. They are meaningful practice. In some schools or districts, routines may be recognized as *math talks*.

Routines Support Reasoning in Mathematics

Reasoning can be thought of as the process of drawing conclusions based on evidence or stated assumptions. Although reasoning is an important part of all disciplines, it plays a special and fundamental role in mathematics. In middle and high school mathematics, reasoning is often understood as engaging in *formal reasoning*, or formulating proofs, in which students are drawing conclusions logically deduced from assumptions and definitions. However, mathematical reasoning can take many forms, ranging from informal explanation and justification to formal deduction, as well as inductive observations. Reasoning begins in the earliest grades. It starts with explorations, various conjectures, false starts, and partial explanations before there is ever a result.

Reasoning is compromised as students accept rule and procedure without investigation of *why?* They then practice these rules and procedures so much that the mathematics and reasoning within them fades away. Their task-at-hand becomes nothing more than completing a collection of problems or steps. Over time, they generalize that *this* is what it means to do mathematics.

Today, technology makes it possible to solve or complete most any calculation quickly. But, how do students know that the result is reasonable? How do they know that a solution displayed on a calculator, tablet, or phone is correct? Determining reasonableness is a collection of abilities and skills, which are much different from procedural calculation. These skills include critical thinking, reasoning, problem solving, and communicating. In fact, these more complex skills are more desirable by Fortune 500 companies than those skills, such as calculation, that were once considered desirable (Boaler, 2015).

Number routines proposed here help students develop complex, essential skills through daily, engaging activities that represent quality practice. The strategies, approaches, and reasoning that they develop during these routines will serve them for a lifetime of everyday mathematics.

Routines Improve Number Sense and Fluency

The National Council of Teachers of Mathematics identifies five components of number sense including number meaning, number relationships, number magnitude, operations involving numbers, and referents for numbers and quantities (NCTM, 2000). Fennell and Landis (1994) describe number sense as "an awareness and understanding about what numbers are, their relationships, their magnitude, the relative effect of operating on numbers, including the use of mental mathematics and estimation" (p. 187). Students with number sense understand relationships between numbers. They estimate. They make use of the properties of operations. They manipulate. Fennell and Landis also describe number sense as "the foundation from which all other mathematical concepts and ideas arise" (p. 188). And, every mathematics teacher relates to their noting that "students with number sense show a good intuition about numbers and their relationships" (p. 187).

Fluency is much more than the quick recall of basic facts. Fluency is being accurate, efficient, and flexible with thinking and computation (National Research Council, 2001). Students show it when they add up or subtract to find the difference between two numbers. They show it when they think about 109 + 43 as 110 + 42. They might show it through their ease of effort when completing a procedure. But, we should also help them pursue it as mental mathematics.

Fluency is more than memorization. We are fluent in all sorts of things that we didn't memorize how to do. For example, we might think of fluency when we think about driving a car. Yet, we don't memorize how to drive a car. Instead, we learn the concept, the rules, and the patterns. We practice and practice. We understand what it means to drive in a variety of places and contexts from parking lots and freeways to sunny days and snow storms. Like driving, fluency with reading, golfing, or doing mathematics is grounded in understanding and rich, diverse practice.

There is likely no correlation between the number of problems on a page and the level of one's fluency or number sense. Students don't develop these skills by completing a certain quantity of problems. Instead, teachers can help students develop them through rich, engaging problems and tasks, through exposure to others' sense and reasoning, and with sound understanding and lots of opportunity for meaningful practice. Routines can be part of that opportunity.

Number sense and fluency extend far beyond whole numbers and basic facts to fractions, decimals, ratio, percent, and much more. Most, if not all, mathematics teachers would identify number sense and fluency as two of the things that matter most. They might also identify them as two of the biggest challenges their students face in mathematics. Because of this, number sense and fluency are the targets of every routine within this book.

Routines Help Fluency Develop Over Time

The mathematical *big ideas* the routines support in this book are critical. They involve concepts and essential skills having to do with counting, magnitude, estimation, and operation sense. Students cannot truly develop or fully understand these ideas in a single unit of study or just a week or two of instruction. Mastery evolves. Students develop mastery over long periods, through frequent use and application in varied situations. They develop mastery through discussion and through brief, consistent, engaging, and meaningful practice. Daily routines enable students to develop, practice, and reinforce understanding of essential skills and concepts over time.

In his book *Outliers*, Malcolm Gladwell suggests that a person needs 10,000 hours of deliberate practice to master something (Gladwell, 2008). Though one might argue the exact amount of time, it is logical that the more people do something—the more they practice and experience something—the better they can understand and apply it. Consider playing an instrument. Passing a written test about the parts of the instrument, the way to hold it, and the meaning of recorded notes doesn't mean someone is proficient with the instrument. Instead, it shows that they understand how the instrument works and the basics of how music is recorded on paper. Their ability to play the instrument, and to play it well, is improved and enhanced as they play it more and more.

This analogy could be applied to number sense and reasoning. The theory here is that with foundational understanding and frequent, plentiful opportunities to practice, students can develop noticeable sense of number, reasoning, and justification. One might note that 10,000 hours seems impossible with limited instructional time and considerable skills and concepts already identified in your curriculum. However, with routines such as these presented, students can achieve a grand amount of *hours on the road* in just a few minutes a day. Consider this, students could access 11,700 minutes of number sense practice through five minutes a day, for 180 days (in a school year), over a 13-year school career. That's 195 hours—or more than one instructional year—for just number sense and reasoning!

Routines Satisfy the Need for Quality Practice

Quality practice is not defined by the number of problems students complete, the speed at which they calculate or recall, nor the number of hours they spend doing mathematics. It is defined by what students do and how they are engaged. Quality practice should engage students in thinking. We mean for the routines in this book to provide quality practice. They offer unique, engaging, and diverse experiences that will help students develop their thinking skills. They are not repetitive nor mundane. They are not mindless drills. These routines provide the quality practice that can help our students perform better in class, outside the mathematics classroom, and even better on standardized tests.

Routines Improve Performance and Achievement

Data from 13 million students who took PISA tests showed that the lowest achieving students worldwide were those who used a memorization strategy (Boaler, 2015, May 7). Simply, thinking and making connections improves student success on standardized tests. Mental computation and estimation can improve students' speed and overall performance. This makes most sense when we consider that test makers design distractors to mimic students' most common computational errors. It makes sense students who estimate, discount possibilities, make decisions about reasonable answers, will reconsider their solutions when choices don't match solutions. Routines that develop reasoning and number sense help students gain confidence, practice thinking, and likely improve overall performance on standardized assessments.

Routines Prevent or Rehabilitate Number Pluckers, Pluggers, and Crunchers

One might say that traditional mathematics instruction has created a *bunch of pluckers*. These pluckers are students who pluck key words or numbers from problems without thinking. It has created *pluggers* who plug numbers into formulas and equations without thinking. It has created *crunchers* who crunch numbers and blindly rely on the results as being correct. The creation of these pluckers, pluggers, and crunchers doesn't happen by accident. It happens when students don't fully understand mathematics concepts. It happens when they are introduced to steps and procedures for generating answers or completing the exercises. It isn't always the result of years of experience. Pluckers and pluggers can begin to appear in early elementary grades.

Success can be fleeting for many, if not all, of the pluckers, pluggers, and crunchers. Their ability to complete a procedure without understanding can, and often is, lost without considerable practice and maintenance. Even then, proficiency can fade. Yet understanding is not lost. When students understand concepts, connect them to procedures, refine their understanding, and transfer it to new situations they show that they never lose it. Routines build on their conceptual understanding, allow students to connect ideas, refine them, and transfer them to new situations. Routines build number sense and fluency. Routines can rehabilitate these students so that they rely on their own thinking instead of or in addition to someone else's rules and procedures.

Routines Encourage a Growth Mindset

The idea of consistent, engaging practice to develop students' number sense and reasoning promotes other prominent ideas about teaching and learning. One of those is a growth mindset. A growth mindset is an approach to teaching mathematics that emphasizes that mindset is more important than initial ability in determining the progress students can make in their mathematical understanding. Students with a growth mindset will make better progress than those with a fixed mindset. Having a growth mindset means:

- believing that talents can be developed and great abilities can be built over time;
- viewing mistakes as an opportunity to develop understanding;
- being resilient;
- believing that effort creates success; and
- thinking about how one learns.

Carol Dweck's work establishes that a growth mindset benefits students by empowering them to develop skills through dedication and hard work. To do this, we must provide them with worthwhile opportunities to engage in and discuss reasoning. Daily routines to work with interesting activities, to build number sense, and to improve reasoning about number and operation naturally complements the facets of a growth mindset. Routines reinforce that students' ability can be developed through continued practice and effort. They help students build confidence. They can undercut any students' notion that their mathematics ability is fixed.

Routines Honor and Leverage Errors

A growth mindset is grounded in making and honoring mistakes. Honoring mistakes is much more than saying that it's ok to make a mistake in class. Honoring mistakes means that mistakes are explored. As Jo Boaler notes, mistakes help grow our brains (Boaler, 2015). Routines are an opportunity for students to reason and make mistakes when doing so. Discussion about reasoning and mistakes help students advance their understanding. As teachers facilitate discussions during routines, it is critical to pursue not only accurate and efficient reasoning but flawed reasoning as well. Exploring students' reasoning and errors tells students that mistakes are more than ok. It tells them that mistakes are valued.

Many people know, it is more powerful to find one's own mistake rather than being told that one is incorrect. During discussion with partners and the class as a whole, students have the opportunity to explain their thinking and thus catch their own mistake. In some cases, exposure to others' reasoning and even others' errors helps students better understand their own reasoning and misconceptions. This can happen at any point during a math class. Starting with a routine built on reasoning and discussion increases, if not guarantees, the likelihood of discussion and exploration of errors or misconceptions.

Routines Actively Develop Confidence

Blindly applying rules to mathematics without understanding can undermine a student's confidence (Van de Walle, 2019) as they rely on disconnected steps without understanding. Stalled fluency erodes confidence. Perceptions of failure associated with making mistakes in mathematics or perceptions of *not having a math gene* damage student confidence. Infrequent, disengaging, or disconnected practice challenge confidence. Yet, jump-start routines can counter each of these challenges and in time enhance students' confidence in themselves and mathematics in general.

IMPLEMENTING JUMP-START ROUTINES

These routines are intended as practical ideas for jump-starting your mathematics class. You can modify them to work with any number concept and most any mathematics concept in general. You can adjust them to fit any amount of time you allocate to begin mathematics class. You can use them with any level of student proficiency in mathematics or any level of student experience with routines. As you implement them, routines become a rich opportunity for meaningful discourse in mathematics and windows into student thinking.

Routines That Are Ready-For-Use

The routines provided throughout the book are ready-for-use. You'll find examples of specific numbers, operations, or concepts along with implementation guidance. These are followed by variations and ideas for how the content might be modified to meet the needs of all elementary content. Each routine is available as a downloadable set of PowerPoint slides.

 All routines can be downloaded for your use at **resources.corwin .com/jumpstartroutines/elementary**

Each can be edited or modified as needed for any classroom. You can copy the slides so that a routine can be extended to the number types or concepts you want to focus on.

Flexible Use

The routines presented here are intended to support high-quality mathematics instruction. There are no specific requirements. You can adjust the time allotted to a routine for all sorts of needs. You can adjust the number of prompts. You can use any routine, in any order, on any day. We offer ideas for using and adjusting routines throughout this book, but there are likely many other ways to adjust a routine. Simply, you can modify any routine however you see fit.

Timing of Routines: How Long? When?

You can manage how long routines last by adjusting the number of questions you ask or the number of student approaches you investigate. You can limit the number of problems or situations that students encounter. You can modify the complexity of the mathematics you present. You can cut or extend the amount of time students have to share their thinking with partners. Essentially, you control the amount of time allocated to your routine. A guide for facilitating a routine might be:

- Students work with the prompt independently (about one minute).
- Students discuss their reasoning with a partner or triad (about two minutes).
- Teacher facilitates class discussion about strategies and reasoning (about three to four minutes).

That said, here are a couple of basic guidelines:

1. These routines are intended to be quick, engaging activities that foster number sense and reasoning. Typically, they should be no more than a few minutes. Most days they should last about five to seven minutes. Other days, they may be a bit more than five minutes. Occasionally, the discussion may be so vibrant and engaging that you find your class spending 10 minutes with the routine. The latter may not be ideal due to time and schedule challenges. However, it's important to note that it may happen from time to time. It's also important to note that these rich discussions are exactly what you want for your students and so spending a few minutes more with them shouldn't be thought of as time lost or wasted.

2. Routines are likely best situated at the beginning of the mathematics class. You can establish protocols for students to enter class and prepare for the

opening routine. In this way, they naturally replace mundane warmups or review of homework. However, you can flexibly position routines throughout the class as well. In longer classes (75 minutes or more), you may decide that they are best used in the middle of the block as an opportunity for rekindling students' energy and engagement. In other cases, you may find that routines can be useful when offered at the end of the class. If you select the end of class, you must be sure to close instruction for the period early enough for the routine to take place. There is an obvious challenge of running out of time when planning for routines at the end of class.

3. Routines may take longer at first. For some students, this is the first time they are consistently challenged to think about mathematics in their own way. For others, discussing their reasoning may be problematic. For you, facilitating and investigating without lingering too long will take some practice. A routine will become more fluid the more you use it. You might experience a *time bump* each instance in which you introduce a new routine. It's important to keep in mind that you control the first minutes of mathematics class. You can extend or limit prompts and discussion to meet the needs of your students and/or the timelines of their lessons.

Which Routines to Use?

There is a selection of varied routines offered here for use in the classroom. There is no suggestion of which to use, when to use it, or how to order the routines. There is no requirement for length of use or timing within the quarter or semester. The recommendation is to use routines that are most comfortable to facilitate and most interesting for your students to investigate. You should select a routine and use it for a few days or weeks before moving to another. You may circle back to the first routine after students have experienced other routines. It's important to remember that any routine can become stale with too much use. You can make subtle adjustments to the routine to keep it fresh. Even so, it will be wise to change out routines as needed.

The Routines At-A-Glance section on page 18–19 offers a table of routines that notes a brief description of the routine and its *purpose*. The purposes connect with aspects of number sense from basic counting strategies, to magnitude of number, number relationships, decomposition, estimation, and operational sense. Regardless of purpose, you can adjust a routine to accommodate the type and size of numbers students have been exposed to. Likewise, Appendix A is a handy look at how each routine meets various purposes and Standards for Mathematical Practice.

Every class is different, and so, it is difficult to say which routines are *best* to begin with. That being said, *Math Yapper* and *Picture It* are two routines that every student can access with minimal proficiency with skills or concepts. These two routines are also attractive options because they are very interesting and highly engaging. Other routines in the first 11 are also good places for you to begin as they feature foundational concepts of counting, number, number relationships, and decomposition.

PLAN FOR THE ROUTINE

While you should focus most of your planning energy on the core skill and concepts of the main lesson, you can incorporate short warm-up routines easily because they are designed for low-intensity planning. They are designed to be replicated with minimal change to develop student number sense and reasoning. You should be able to change out skills and concepts within the routine with little effort. However, there are some things to keep in mind when selecting and planning the routine.

Select the Routine and the Content or Concepts

Obviously, you need to know how to facilitate the routine. You must understand the basic tenets of the routine. You must also select skills and concepts that are appropriate for your students. You must decide if you want to feature whole numbers or operations. You will need to determine if your students need help with operational sense or more general number sense. Experience informs this. But, you also might take cues from class discussion, student work, or test results about what topics and ideas need to be developed. Armed with this information, you can prepare the routine.

- Routines for Foundations of Counting: These routines develop ideas about counting. The routines have students count, estimate, and represent counting. These routines can be modified for skip-counting, counting with fractions, and counting with decimals.

- Routines for Magnitude and Context of Number: These routines develop students' sense of magnitude and the meaning of numbers in context. Students estimate and reason about quantity in these routines.

- Routines for Number Relationships: These routines develop a diverse collection of ideas about numbers. They investigate decomposition and representation of numbers, including number lines.

- Routines for Operational Sense and Estimation: These routines examine patterns and relationships within operations. These routines also highlight estimation of operations to determine reasonableness of solutions.

Scaffolding to Support Routines

Routines are intended to be mental mathematics activities. Students should have background understanding for these quality opportunities to practice mathematics. You can provide tools to support students as needed. At the least, you and your students can use tools to support discussion and confirm accuracy of calculations and reasoning. Tools you might consider providing include:

- calculators for students to confirm accurate calculations and explore patterns;

- number charts for students to confirm accurate calculations and explore patterns;

- fact charts for students to make accurate calculations when recall isn't fully established;

- base 10 models, including but not limited to base 10 blocks and 10 frames, to anchor student understanding and support justifications;

- anchor charts for students to access so that they can be reminded of learned strategies, relationships, or representations; and

- personal dry erase boards, sticky notes, or journals for students to record their thinking and to use to support them when communicating ideas.

Other ways you can support student success is to identify and target numbers that students can work with well. Students learning about three-digit numbers may be best served by using routines that featured two-digit numbers. Routines are not intended as tools of first instruction.

Anchor References and Tools

Student reasoning and conversation can be buoyed by anchor references during routines. These references are tools or charts that help them make sense of concepts, confirm accuracy of their calculations, or frame their arguments. These tools might be anchor charts that can be referenced during discussion. For example, an anchor chart that reinforces decomposition of addends might be referred to as students talk about how they found compatible addends in the routine *Make It Friendly* (page 76). Other tools such as personal 10 frames can help students represent combinations of 10 or how to use 10 when adding or subtracting.

Students might have personal tools. Personal hundred charts, addition charts, multiplication charts, or calculators can support accuracy. They may be used for students who are still mastering basic facts or in cases where students are developing proficiency with adding two-digit numbers. These accuracy tools may be needed for two important reasons. First, and most obviously, they help provide checks and balances to ensure accuracy when counting and computing. They also help some students access the rich activities that these routines are. Brains are challenged to do two complex things at once. The reasoning needed for these routines competes with the need to calculate. These tools can alleviate some of that challenge. As students' accuracy and precision grows, you can begin to limit or remove these tools. Even so, they should always be available to confirm that strategies and approaches are accurate.

Other personal tools might include paper and pencil or personal white boards or lapboards. These tools are fine for students to jot down ideas, sketch models of problems, and so on. However, routines are intended to develop students' fluency and mental mathematics skills. Providing these tools sends messages that counter the intent. Instead of making these tools available initially, you might choose to direct your students to them when you misjudged the numbers, concepts, or reasoning in a routine and students need support to work through it.

Anchor charts can be extended beyond concepts. They might also capture vocabulary and sentence starters to help students make arguments or rebut classmates. Vocabulary anchor charts might be situated near the projection of the routine so that statements can be made with precise mathematical language. Keep in mind that posting the charts alone will not ensure that students use the language. Instead, you can revoice student statements and inject the accurate vocabulary while referring to the chart.

Vocabulary charts can be complemented with sentence starter posters. Sentence starters are familiar tools in elementary schools. They help students make clear statements. They help students think about how to begin their declarations. They also help students respond to statements of classmates and their teachers. There is no one set of starters that is better than another. Below are some helpful examples. You might edit these prompts, add to them, or eliminate some altogether. Help starters include:

I think that _____ because …

I decided that …

I chose _____ because …

I agree with ___ because …

I disagree with ___ because …

I think ___'s idea will always work because …

The pattern I noticed was …

My thinking will always work because …

I want to change my answer because …

Listen for charts are anchor charts that help students determine what to listen for in someone's argument. They might be single words or indicators such as *clarity, vocabulary*, or *make sense*. Listen for charts might also be questions or prompts that ask the listener questions such as *is the argument clear, are math words being used*, or *does the idea make sense*? These listen for charts also help students think about what they might say before they say it.

It is important to keep a few things in mind about anchor references you or your students use during routines or instruction in general. First and foremost, students need explicit instruction about these charts and the tools. Students must understand how the mathematics tools work. Students should discuss when it is a good idea to use a tool or refer to a chart. And, anchor charts about concepts or discussion techniques should be developed *with* students instead of simply displayed *to* students.

How to Structure the Conversation

Jump-start routines intend to develop number sense and reasoning. Developing reasoning and number sense is not done in isolation. It is not the sole result of endless hours of practice or drill and kill. Our thinking about numbers is developed by the exposure to and exchange of ideas. Exchanges are student to student, student to teacher, and of course teacher to student. They are discussion and conversation.

Routines and the conversations within them should take on a familiar structure so that the endeavor becomes, well, routine. Prompts are posed. Students engage in the prompt. Students share ideas with partners so that all have an opportunity to talk. Then, a group conversation is had. During that time, every student does not have to share out. You don't have to explore every strategy. You don't have to discuss every solution.

You make choices about what to explore, where to linger, and when to move on during the debrief. You facilitate discussion. You ask questions. From time to time, you will have to insert an idea or strategy. However, routines aren't intended to be mini-lessons or mini-lectures on a procedure that students are to carry out and practice. Conversation during routines is an opportunity for meaningful discourse.

How to Set the Stage for Meaningful Discourse

Because discussion is such a critical component of the routines in this book, Smith and Stein's five practices for orchestrating productive discussions naturally outline how we can plan for routines. These practices remind us to anticipate, monitor, select, sequence, and connect (Smith & Stein, 2018).

1. Anticipate What Students Might Do During the Routine

Anticipating what students might do helps you consider how you will respond intentionally rather than randomly. Considering student ideas and misconceptions can also help you think about other prompts you might pose through the routine in subsequent days. You can start anticipating simply by thinking about how you would find the solution to the prompt. Throughout this book, you will find routines with particular skills and concepts, many of which share some of the reasoning and solutions your students may offer.

2. Monitor Student Discussions During the Routine

Monitor means that you listen to students as they work on a problem or discuss their thinking, particularly when discussing them with a partner or small group. Granted, it is unlikely that you can listen to every student conversation. However, you can be strategic about the discussions we monitor. You may monitor the discussion of targeted concerns. You may monitor discussions of students that have shown inconsistent performance with a specific skill or concept. You may plan to monitor different groups on different days to balance whose conversations you listen to and focus on.

3. Select Strategy and Reasoning to Promote During the Routine

As with discussions during your core lesson, you have to be careful not to randomly select students for discussion during routines. A random selection may compromise the discussion. Anticipating what students might do or think during the routine can help you think about the conversations or ideas that you want to listen for when monitoring. This coupled with considering the strategies, reasoning, or possible misconceptions that we want to highlight can help us select students for sharing during whole group discussion of the routine.

4. Sequence Ideas During the Routine

Strategies and ideas should be sequenced during discussion to advance student understanding. Sequencing may be most challenging during a routine. In fact, careful, deliberate sequencing of ideas during a routine may be impossible due to the time constraints or inability to monitor every discussion in the short amount of time. We may be able to offset some of the sequencing challenge with our questions. To do this, we can pose questions that help students make connections between strategies, reflect on efficiency, and make use of structure and patterns within prompts. These questions might include:

- How is ____'s strategy similar to ____'s?
- How is ___'s strategy different than ___'s?
- How does this idea connect to something we have discussed recently?
- Will this approach always work?
- If we think about efficiency, how do these strategies compare?
- What patterns do you notice in the expressions?
- How did you use patterns to help you find your solution?

5. Connect Strategies and Concepts During the Routine

Your questions during routines should help students connect solution paths or varied reasoning. Your questions should help students see connections between concepts. You should also help students make connections between numbers, operations, and representations. You may even make decisions on the fly to extend student reasoning to new situations or problems through your questions. We offer questions for each routine in this book to support and guide you in facilitating discussion and connecting strategies, skills, or concepts.

PRACTICAL ADVICE FOR ROUTINES

Routines can be a component of your instruction that should require very little preparation. They should be both useful and practical. You should use them in ways that complement who you are as a teacher, what you value in mathematics, and what your students need. We note some important advice for working with routines below.

Modify, Modify, Modify

Routines work with any skill or concept. You can change the content to match the needs of your students. Change it to meet a specific purpose. Modify how the routine functions. There are ideas presented here about how a routine should unfold, but this is only a guide. Consistently monitor how students interact with the routine. Compare their work with the intent. Adjust or modify as needed.

Identify or Create the Content or Topics

Identifying or creating the content for the routines may be the most complicated aspect of routines. The topics should be those that students need to further develop or refine. There are many examples and modifications offered throughout this book to ease that challenge. Yet, there are other resources for creating examples. The prime resource is your students themselves. Having students create the number prompts may offer added benefit as it gives them an opportunity for thinking deeply about the identified concept. You can have students write or create routine situations as a homework assignment. You might also have students create routine situations as independent work once they have completed an in-class assignment. Keep in mind that students should work with a routine before creating prompts or problems for it. Also keep in mind that students can design quite creative, complicated, or unique situations.

Use Routines Formatively

Routines are a good way to formatively assess students. They can help you determine student perspectives and reasoning. They can help you monitor student proficiency with skills and concepts that they previously learned. They might help you determine specific types of numbers and operations that you might reteach or revisit through mini-lessons and other activities.

Be Committed and Creative

It's possible that the first few times you use a routine you find the activity to be clunky. This is natural. Try to give the routine some time before cutting ties with it. You can also reflect on how you can make it better or how you might modify the content or process to improve its effectiveness. Be mindful, too, that reasoning, communicating about reasoning, and working with mathematics mentally may be new to your students. Because of this, it may take some time for them to get comfortable with a routine. As noted, you can creatively adjust or modify the routine to best meet the needs of your students and your style of instruction.

JUMP-START ROUTINES AT-A-GLANCE

	ROUTINE	DESCRIPTION	PURPOSE
1	Math Yapper	Students provide clues for partners to guess mystery numbers, concepts, or vocabulary.	Develop understanding of concepts and vocabulary to communicate clearly.
2	The Count	Students make predictions about counting when given starting points and an interval.	Develop counting and skip-counting skills and estimation.
3	The Missing	Students determine missing numbers on a number chart.	Develop advanced strategies about counting.
4	Big or Small	Students determine when a number represents something big and when a number represents something small.	Develop sense of quantity and magnitude through contexts for number.
5	Picture It	Students estimate quantities in pictures.	Develop understanding of magnitude of numbers by reasoning about them in context.
6	Show It 3	Students represent a number in three diverse ways.	Develop deeper understanding of single and multi-digit number concepts.
7	How Can You Make It?	Students determine ways to make a number.	Develop understanding of number composition and decomposition.
8	The Mighty Ten	Students find combinations of 10, multiples of 10, 100, or 1,000.	Develop fluency with combinations of ten and transfer this fluency to multi-digit numbers.
9	Make It Friendly	Students add more than one number by finding friendly numbers.	Develop strategies for adding and subtracting numbers using decomposition and compatible numbers.
10	Mystery Number	Students use clues about a number to determine if they have the mystery number.	Develop understanding about number through attributes and relationships.
11	Number Bio	Students complete prompts about a given number.	Develop understanding about numbers through representations, attributes, and relationships.
12	Condition	Students use conditions about a number to earn points.	Develop understanding of number and flexibility of reasoning.
13	Where's the Point?	Students determine possible values for unknown locations on empty number lines.	Develop understanding of number relationships with number lines.

	ROUTINE	DESCRIPTION	PURPOSE
14	*Is This the End?*	Students determine endpoints for a number line when the value of a certain location is known.	Develop understanding of number relationships with number lines.
15	*About or Between*	Students estimate sums, differences, products, and quotients.	Develop estimation strategies for determining if computation results are reasonable.
16	*More or Less*	Students compare expressions to a known value.	Reinforce computational fluency by estimating and determining reasonable answers.
17	*This or That?*	Students compare expressions by reasoning about patterns and properties of operations.	Deepen understanding of patterns and relationships within operations and the properties of operations.
18	*Finding One and All*	Students use a known computation to find unknowns in related equations.	Develop strategies for computing flexibly and efficiently.
19	*Another Way to Say It*	Students rethink or rewrite expressions to find results more efficiently.	Develop strategies for computing flexibly and efficiently.
20	*The Truth*	Students consider if equations are true or false.	Reinforce understanding of operations and the meaning of the equal sign.

NOTES

PART 2

JUMP-START ROUTINES

VIDEO DEMONSTRATIONS:

 The Count

 The Missing

 Big or Small

 Show It 3

 How Can You Make It?

 Condition

 Where's the Point?

 Is This the End?

 More or Less

 This or That?

 Another Way to Say It

 The Truth

 All videos can be viewed at **resources.corwin.com/jumpstartroutines/elementary**

MATH YAPPER (COMMUNICATING ABOUT MATH)

About the Routine

A rhombus is not a diamond. An expression is not an equation, and there is a difference between lines and line segments. We cannot overemphasize the importance of vocabulary in our world, especially in mathematics. As students, many of us worked to memorize definitions of vocabulary terms. Some of us may recall copying definitions three times or taking quizzes in which we matched terms and definitions. But as we know, true mastery is much more. We want our students to share ideas with accurate vocabulary. We want them to understand meaning, application, and relationship within terms. We want them to retain and use the vocabulary. This happens through multiple exposures over time. It happens through engaging opportunities for practice and play. *Math Yapper* is a routine to do just that. In it, students describe mystery terms to partners so that their partner can identify the term. The activity is

> Sum
>
> Triangle

similar to the gameshow *$20,000 Pyramid* or the board game Hedbanz™. The goal of the routine is to get your partner to say the mystery terms before others in the class. After individual pairs play, clues are shared with the class.

Why It Matters

This routine helps students:

- communicate meaning of mathematics vocabulary accurately (MP6);

- consider varied aspects of mathematics vocabulary, including associated words, non-examples, and other uses of the vocabulary;

- listen to the ideas of others to make meaning (MP3);

- compare and contrast their understanding of vocabulary with others;

- process feedback to consider different strategies or approaches;

online resources ↘ All tasks can be downloaded for your use at **resources.corwin.com/ jumpstartroutines/elementary**

- find alternative ways to communicate and find solutions (MP1);
- ask themselves if a definition or description is reasonable (MP6); and
- defend their reasoning and the approaches of others (MP3).

What They Should Understand First

Students are prepared to engage in this routine regardless of their grade or class level. Simply, any mathematics vocabulary from current units or previous learning can be used. Images and various representations also work well. Even so, students should have opportunities to explore vocabulary prior to the routine. Opportunities for practice include completing graphic organizers to consider different facets of a term. In this Frayer example, students write a definition, think of related words, examples, and non-examples, for *addition*. In another activity, students web any and all ideas connected to a vocabulary term. It is critical that you use vocabulary frequently and accurately in your classroom. Use of lay terms may be unavoidable or

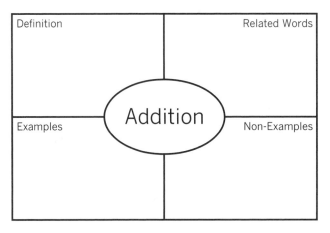

accidental, but when it happens, you should pause and correct the term before continuing.

What to Do

1. Select terms to use for the routine. Terms do not have to be associated with each other or the current unit of study. The number of terms to pose is dependent upon the amount of time allocated to the routine.

2. Assign partners and ask them to stand.

3. Arrange partners so that one faces the board or screen and the other faces away from it.

4. Direct students facing the screen to give clues to their partners about the terms being displayed.

5. Remind students that they cannot say exactly what appears on the screen.

6. Direct students to sit down as soon as their partner guesses both terms.

7. Circulate as students give clues listening for perspective and misunderstanding.

8. Facilitate a discussion about clues and interpretations after the game is complete.

Here are some questions for the term *sum* (in the featured example) you might ask:

» How did you describe *sum* to your partner?

» What other ways could we describe a *sum*?

» What are examples of a sum?

» When do we work with sums in class?

» Are any other ideas similar to or different from a sum?

» Where else might we hear the term *sum*?

» How is that use similar or different than the mathematical meaning of *sum*?

9. Optional: Record student ideas about clues on the screen.

10. Honor and explore both accurate and flawed clues.

Frayer Model Source: Adapted from: "A Schema for Testing the Level of Concept Mastery" by D. A. Frayer, W. C. Frederick, & H. G. Klausmeier, Technical Report No. 16. Copyright 1969 by the University of Wisconsin.

Anticipated Strategies for This Example

```
Sum

Triangle
```

The debrief is an opportunity to uncover student thinking and perception. You might hear students describe *sum* (from the example) as the answer to an addition problem. Others might say that it is what you get when you add two numbers or possibly two addends. Some students might use an example such as 4 + 4 = 8. They might connect the word to non-mathematical terms trying to communicate *some* rather than *sum*. During the whole-class debrief, it is important to highlight how each of these ideas applies to the term *sum*. Your job is to help students connect descriptions and examples. In some cases, such as triangle (from the example), students might use gestures. This is a viable and appropriate strategy. But, it is important that you highlight how the gesture is related to the meaning of the term. Student misunderstanding or imprecision can occur. This is an opportunity to help students correct their thinking by making connections, refining their understanding, and reinforcing accurate terminology.

MATH YAPPER—ADDITIONAL EXAMPLES

A. *Math Yapper* can feature related or unrelated terms or topics. Example A features the related terms *numerator* and *equivalent fractions*. Related terms can help determine if students recognize and leverage the relationship between terms. In this example, they might share clues to establish what a numerator is. Be sure to listen for student preference of definitions or examples. In this case you might hear that the numerator is the top number. Though accurate, there are other ways to think about it especially when related to equivalent fractions. With related terms, students might use the first term to establish the second. You might hear that a numerator doubles when a denominator doubles for communicating equivalent fractions.

```
A

Numerator

Equivalent Fractions
```

NOTES

_____

_____

_____

_____

_____

_____

_____

B. *Math Yapper* can be used to reinforce terms from previous units or grades. Terms might even be used before an upcoming unit to get a sense of what students have retained from previous instruction. The terms offered to students do not have to be connected. Example B presents *product* and *rhombus*. These terms—and even the units in which they appear—aren't related. Returning to terms throughout the year—especially essential terms—such as product, helps students retain the term and its meaning. It increases the likelihood that students will use the term in other contexts when appropriate. There is no rule as to when unrelated terms might be sprinkled in. Instead, you might make a mental note when a student doesn't recall the term during class or uses descriptors instead of the exact term (e.g., answer instead of product). In the following days, you might then feature that term during the routine.

B

Product

Rhombus

C. *Math Yapper* isn't limited to two terms per round. You can adjust it for three or more terms. What is important is that it doesn't take too much time from focused instruction. It should be just a few minutes to jump-start the beginning of class. It's also important to engage students in both giving and receiving clues. Because of this, you should be careful to limit the number of examples used. You might consider using terms from your mathematics *word wall* during *Math Yapper*. The three terms used in Example C are related. They even build upon one another as a *digit* is something used within a *place value* and the *hundreds place* is an example of *place value*. As noted in Example B, the three terms don't have to be related. Yet when related, there is potential for creating a stronger bond in students' mental vocabulary network.

C

Digit

Place Value

Hundreds Place

D. The need for precision when communicating cannot be disputed. Nor can one discount the role that vocabulary plays in this precision. But, it's also important to communicate about numbers precisely. You can do this with expressions, relationships, calculations, or features such as place value. Students should think about numbers flexibly, but in this version of *Math Yapper*, students will think *and* communicate about numbers flexibly. For 814, students might share that it is one more than 815 or 10 less than 824. They might think of it as twice as much as 407 or 15 more than 799. As students show preference for a certain clue, such as one more or one less, you can place restrictions on what types of clues can or cannot be used. This helps students expand their understanding of what numbers are and how they are related.

D
814
75

NOTES

MATH YAPPER VARIATION—COMPUTATION

You can change representations of numbers or quantities as students become more comfortable communicating about mathematics. You can make these adjustments to develop basic fact recall or other patterns and relationships within computations. These changes serve other purposes as well. They provide opportunity for alternative forms of assessment providing insight into student strategies.

E. Consider Example E. How would your students communicate 7 + 9 to a classmate? Would they recall the sum and ask for addition facts that have the same sum? This would work. However, they might use related facts. For example, 7 + 9 is related to 6 + 10. Using this clue, students demonstrate that they can find the sum, but more importantly, they recognize relationships between addends. Often, highlighting this clue during the class debrief will help other students either acquire or reinforce a skill, relationship, or concept. You can expand and strengthen the relationships by exposing other clues or even offering your own. 7 + 9 is related to 10 + 6. But, it is also related to 8 + 8. It helps students understand that an amount can be given from the first to the second addend or vice versa. You can adjust such prompts to any fact set or operation.

E

$$7 + 9$$

$$4 + 6$$

F. Example E shows how you might use facts with unknown sums. But, students can also engage in the routine from the *opposite* direction. Example F shows what that might look like. Here, students are given a value and directed to describe it with a specific operation. For *24 (only ×)* students are directed to communicate 24 using only multiplication. So, students might use 8 × 3, 4 × 6, or 2 × 12. Students who say 24 × 1 are mathematically correct but break the rules of the routine by saying *24*. You could modify the example to work with quotients. To do so, you might give a prompt such as *5 (only ÷)*. Students would then have to give division clues, such as 20 ÷ 4, to get their partner to say *5*. As with Example E, this variation of *Math Yapper* works with any operation or fact set.

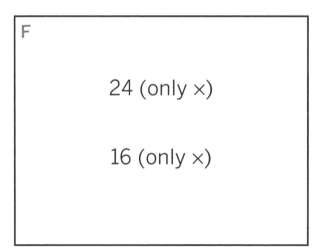

F

$$24 \text{ (only ×)}$$

$$16 \text{ (only ×)}$$

MATH YAPPER VARIATION—IMAGES

Math Yapper might be challenging for young elementary students still learning to read. You can modify the routine to feature images of numbers or mathematical concepts instead. When doing so, the clue giver has to interpret what the picture means and then give clues about the picture. As with any routine, it is critical that you model with the class first before using it with them.

G. Example G shows how you might use images of numbers with young students. This example offers food for thought. You may first choose to represent numbers with the same model. Maybe, you show numbers with 10 frames only. Using the same representation over and over again has benefits. It helps students develop understanding and familiarity of the representation. But, the same representation can be varied as well. For example, you can represent four with four dots in the top row with one missing from the right cell. Or, the missing may be the left cell. You can also show four on the bottom row, or as two dots on top of two dots anywhere on the 10 frame, or even a dot in each corner of the 10 frame. Presenting numbers in varied ways will help you understand how your students perceive numbers.

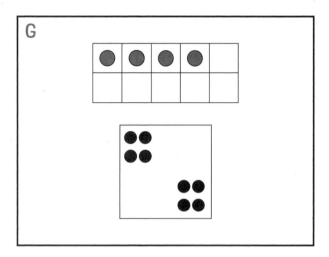

online resources Dot cards (available at resources.corwin.com/jumpstartroutines/elementary) and base 10 blocks are possible representations to use as well. Take a look at the dot card in Example G. This is just one of the many ways to show eight. Varying representations will enrich the discussion as you can highlight the different counting strategies students use.

Mixing up the representations can help students build a deeper understanding of quantity. As in the example, you might mix 10 frames with dot cards. In other examples, you might use base 10 blocks. Number paths and number lines are also good representations for students to decipher.

H. Example H shows how you might feature representations of other mathematical ideas in the routine. The top is an example of how fractions might be used in *Math Yapper*. Here, unrelated concepts are shown simply to broaden examples. Would students see one-fifth or four-fifths? That alone would be a great conversation. In the bottom example, see how you might share geometric figures. Note that more than one triangle is shared. The intent is that students will recognize that both are triangles and give clues so that their partner guesses *triangle*. More than one representation of a concept or term helps students consolidate and generalize meaning.

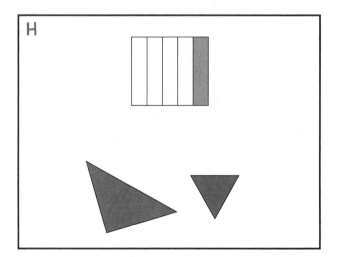

THE COUNT (COUNTING AND SKIP-COUNTING)

About the Routine

Counting is the foundation of mathematics. It is a basic, yet not-so-basic skill. It is a foundation built on five familiar principles of one-to-one, stable-order, cardinality, abstraction, and order-irrelevance (Gelman & Gallistel, 1978). These principles are nurtured co-dependently and refined through practice and experience. And so, counting activities are abundant in primary classrooms. Those experiences can create an artificial, memorized, or ritualistic perspective of counting for students. In other cases, those experiences are lost opportunities for folding in other important ideas about quantity, including estimation. *The Count* is a routine intended to build fluency with counting, practice estimation, and engage students. During the routine, students count by varied intervals. Students predict the results of a counted sequence and compare those results to the actual results. Through continued use, students transfer ideas about one-to-one counting to other intervals and skip-counts. In time, the routine might even be used to develop

fluency of counting backwards by one and other intervals. With intentional recording or connections to charts, the routine can spotlight patterns in the counted numbers. But, *The Count* is much more than a kindergarten routine. By changing intervals to fractions or decimals, it can become a routine for upper elementary students as well.

> Start with 65.
> Count by **ONES**.
>
> What number will we end with?
> What number will you say?

Why It Matters

This routine helps students:

- develop proficiency with counting principles, including one-to-one, stable-order, cardinality, abstraction, and order-irrelevance;

- estimate quantity and results (MP2);
- reason about number and quantity in the real world (MP2);

 All tasks can be downloaded for your use at **resources.corwin.com/ jumpstartroutines/elementary**

- justify if estimated results are reasonable (MP2);
- transfer ideas about counting to other intervals and skip-counts (MP2);
- look for patterns in counting sequences (MP7); and
- communicate their reasoning to others (MP3).

What They Should Understand First

The Count will develop understanding of counting through experience, practice, and repetition. However, students should show understanding of connections between what they are counting and what they are saying (cardinality). They recognize that counting any type of object is the same as counting anything else (abstraction). In fact, you could easily modify this routine to arrange cubes or counters in a pattern and count them instead of students. Students should also show understanding of other counting principles, including one-to-one correspondence, including the notion that a thing can be counted and given a number only once and that there is a stable, repeated order to counting. For young students, this routine should begin with one and count only by ones to establish these principles. As students mature mathematically, you can begin to change the starting number. Even later, you can introduce various intervals or skip-counts (Examples C, D, E, F, G, and H). Predictions or estimations about the ending number will rely on understanding and experience with estimating quantity, though you may wish to withhold this aspect during initial experiences with the routine.

What to Do

1. Arrange students in a line, a u-shaped group, or a circle. (Note: In this routine, you can use counters and other objects displayed or projected with a document camera instead.)
2. Tell students of the interval and starting number for the routine.
3. Identify which student will begin count and who will end it. (Note: The routine does not have to include every student each time. In a group of 20 students, eight students within the group can be identified for the count rather than all 20.)
4. Ask students to make predictions about the count (see questions below).
5. Have students share their predictions with a classmate.
6. Highlight student ideas before the count. You might pose questions like the following through the slide or verbally.
   - » What number do you think the count will end with?
   - » What number do you think you will say?
   - » What other numbers do you think will be said during the count?
   - » How did you think about these predictions?
7. Record student predictions (optional).
8. Have the group complete the count.
9. After the count, discuss the process of counting and/or the predictions before the count. Questions to ask might include:
   - » How does our prediction compare with the actual result?
   - » Were there any numbers that were hard to think about during the count? What was hard to remember about those numbers?
10. Relate predictions and numbers counted to number charts, number lines, or number paths if needed.
11. Provide a new count if time permits. Consider using a related group-size, start number, or sequence.

Anticipated Strategies for This Example

Start with 65.
Count by **ONES**.

What number will we end with?
What number will you say?

Starting with 65 and counting by ones (featured example) is for students who have begun counting from different numbers. Students may be challenged to think about new numbers as they conclude a decade (69) and begin a new decade (70). In these cases, hundred charts may be especially helpful. It is natural that students might use their fingers or other tools to keep track of and to remember the sequence of the count.

Leveraging tools and patterns should be neither admonished nor required. You can direct students challenged to recall a number to tools, including charts or ticked number lines (with numbers). Students may have to repeat a segment of the count to recall their own number. As students predict the last number to be said, teachers might see them quickly counting the entire group or part of the group to get a sense of what that number might be. Others might make predictions at random. Discussion after the routine can help all polish how they make estimates about counting sequences and quantity.

THE COUNT—ADDITIONAL EXAMPLES

A. *The Count* is perfect for work with early counters. Example A shows how it is easily modified for them. Here, students start with 8 and count by ones. Yet, even this modification may be too advanced. It could be adjusted to simply begin with 0 each time until the concept of counting on from a given number is introduced and understood. For this work, it is essential to use tools, including counting paths, number lines, and/or number charts, including 20-charts, 50-charts, and 100-charts. Young counters would benefit from predicting the last number counted and the number they would say. Even so, it might be wise to avoid spending too much time discussing these predictions until sense of quantity and counting is better developed. Of course, this component of the routine can be eliminated until that time as well.

A

Start with 8.
Count by **ONES**.

What number will we end with?
What number will you say?

B. Example B shows a different take on *The Count*. Counting forward is an explicit expectation within primary standards. Counting backwards is not. However, it is a practical extension that can be used with students as appropriate. You might first use this before employing other modification strategies. Those strategies, such as counting on from numbers greater than 100 or 120 are good to use after sound counting skills within 100 are in place. So, Example B might be a nice option in the time between mastery of counting within 100 and counting with numbers greater than 120. As in other instances of the routine, tools can be quite useful for helping students count backwards.

> **B**
>
> ## Start with 93.
> ## Count backward by **ONES**.
>
> What number will we end with?
> What number will you say?

C. *The Count* begins to show its potential in Example C. You can leverage the routine to develop more advanced counting ideas, including skip-counts. Here, students count by fives starting with 50. The starting point of 50 is intentional though it might be better reserved until students show proficiency with skip-counts that begin with 0. Again, charts and other tools can support accuracy and discussion. Yet, with these modifications it is also a good idea to record the numbers as they are said. Recording these numbers without other *number noise* on charts and number lines allows the post-count discussion to focus on patterns within the numbers. It helps students *see* that the ones place of numbers said in a skip-count by fives is always 0 or 5.

> **C**
>
> ## Start with 50.
> ## Count by **FIVES**.
>
> What number will we end with?
> What number will you say?

D. Example D shows how *The Count* can be modified to work with any possibility. Here, students begin with 28 and skip-count by fives. They can predict numbers that they might say, and you might not be surprised to initially hear numbers that have a 0 or 5 in the tens place. As this example plays out in the classroom, you should again record the numbers said in a row or column to discuss the relationships. During discussion, help students make connections within the patterns. For example, you might first skip count by 5 starting with 30 (30, 35, 40, 45, ...), and then do a second skip count by fives starting with 28 (28, 33, 38, 43, ...). Doing so, helps students see that there is a pattern in the ones place and that there is a relationship between the terms (each term is two less in the second count because 28 is two less than 30).

> **D**
>
> ## Start with 28.
> ## Count by **FIVES**.
>
> What number will we end with?
> What number will you say?

THE COUNT VARIATION—UNUSUAL SKIP-COUNTS

Early skip-counting relies on intervals that relate to other concepts in elementary mathematics. Students skip-count by twos helping to learn about even and odd numbers. They work with skip-counts of 5 and 10, which relate to money. Skip-counts with 10, as with hundreds, also support developing concepts of place value. Because students work with these intervals so often, teachers can be led to believe that students have a much better understanding of skip-counting than they really do. In some cases (especially when starting with 0), students have simply memorized a pattern in the numbers similar to memorizing the alphabet. They may not truly understand what it means to skip-count.

E. Example E is an opportunity to extend and enhance student understanding of skip-counting. Here, students begin with 70 and skip-count by 20. In some classrooms, this will be a good place to start. In others, you might start with zero and skip-count by 20. You might do this after counting by twos and then by tens and discussing the relationships in all three patterns. Doing so helps students make connections. It might be most useful to record each of the three skip-counts in adjacent columns so that the relationship is most clear.

> **E**
>
> Start with 70.
> Count by **TWENTIES**.
>
> What number will we end with?
> What number will you say?

F. Skip-counting by other intervals, such as four in Example F, also has benefits. It can provide an opportunity for students to see deeper relationships between numbers. Of course, most primary students recognize that 2 is half of 4. Yet, they might not know how that affects the numbers in a pattern when skip-counting by the two intervals. Recording the results of counting by 2 beside the results of counting by 4 is a way to expose them to these ideas. It can be applied to other variations as well including skip-counts of 4 and 8 or 3 and 6.

> **F**
>
> Start with 48.
> Count by **FOURS**.
>
> What number will we end with?
> What number will you say?

THE COUNT VARIATION—FRACTIONS AND DECIMALS

Skip-counting by unusual skip-counts, like 4 (Example F), can lay the groundwork for work with multiples and divisibility. *The Count* can be varied to take advantage of most any interval. It can be used with fractions and decimals. In these variations, students again count by a specific interval, predict their number or the ending number, and discuss predictions and patterns afterwards.

G. *The Count* is useful for reinforcing the understanding of fractions as numbers. As with whole numbers for young students, it is wise to begin with 0 consistently before shifting to non-0 starting numbers. In Example G, students begin with 0 and count by fourths. Using unit fractions is also a favorable starting place. In time, you can change the interval to non-unit fractions. In those cases, students might count by two-thirds, three-fourths, or two-fifths. In all cases, denominators should remain useful, practical, and/or common, including denominators of halves, fourths, eights, thirds, and fifths.

Work with fractions may rely excessively on fractions less than 1. This may limit student understanding or ability to use mixed numbers. The routine could be varied so that the counting interval uses mixed numbers. For example, students might begin with 0 and count by $1\frac{1}{2}$ or $1\frac{1}{2}$. The starting number can be adjusted to a mixed number as well. Students might be prompted to begin with 1 and a half and count by halves.

H. Decimal counts are a convenient modification for older students as well. As with other situations, students can begin with 0 and count by tenths or hundredths. The pattern within the counting becomes familiar quite quickly. Soon, starting numbers need to be adjusted so that students can deepen their understanding of patterns within counts of tenths and hundredths. In Example H, students begin with 0.29 and count by tenths. Changing the start to such a decimal number reinforces that the number of hundredths doesn't change as one counts (adds or subtracts) by tenths. Again, you can ask students to think about what number they might say and what the last number counted might be.

G

Start with 0.
Count by **FOURTHS**.

What number will we end with?
What number will you say?

H

Start with 0.29.
Count by **TENTHS**.

What number will we end with?
What number will you say?

Tools are helpful for working or counting with decimals as well. Using money and the relationship to it can help students gain familiarity with decimal concepts. However, it can also be problematic as coins and bills are disproportionate. It has other limits, as connections to place value and whole numbers is not always as noticeable, and in some cases, it might lead to a false sense of student understanding. Instead, students might be supported with decimal charts.

The decimal chart shows a clear relationship between the numbers. It also does well to highlight patterns within the various decimal counts. The chart can be easily modified to capture the values between other whole numbers (2 to 3 or 15 to 16) or between tenths so that work with thousandths can be done (0 and 0.1).

.01	.02	.03	.04	.05	.06	.07	.08	.09	.10
.11	.12	.13	.14	.15	.16	.17	.18	.19	.20
.21	.22	.23	.24	.25	.26	.27	.28	.29	.30
.31	.32	.33	.34	.35	.36	.37	.38	.39	.40
.41	.42	.43	.44	.45	.46	.47	.48	.49	.50
.51	.52	.53	.54	.55	.56	.57	.58	.59	.60
.61	.62	.63	.64	.65	.66	.67	.68	.69	.70
.71	.72	.73	.74	.75	.76	.77	.78	.79	.80
.81	.82	.83	.84	.85	.86	.87	.88	.89	.90
.91	.92	.93	.94	.95	.96	.97	.98	.99	1.00

online resources ☝ This chart can be downloaded for your use at **resources.corwin.com/ jumpstartroutines/elementary**

THE MISSING (COUNTING AND SKIP-COUNTING)

About the Routine

Students learn about and use all sorts of tools to help them count and make sense of number relationships. A number chart is one of the most fundamental tools that students work with. Though this tool is instrumental, if not used well, it can undermine student progress toward more complex ideas about numbers and counting. Often, missing numbers on the chart are surrounded by known or completed numbers. In some cases, the entire chart is completed with the exception of a handful of *missing* numbers. Students are then asked to find the missing numbers. Students are likely to simply count on from knowns. Unfortunately, some students may still begin with 1 and count on to find the missing number, even though many of the numbers are already present. There are missed opportunities to discuss other counting strategies, including 10 more and 10 less, two more and two less, and so on. *The Missing* asks students to find

1	2	3	4	5	6	7	8		
						17			
31									
			54						
61									
								80
								90
			95					

specific missing numbers with few markers to offer support. After finding targeted unknowns, students then share how they counted thus exposing others to possibly unknown, unfamiliar, or uncomfortable counting strategies.

Why It Matters

This routine helps students:

- persevere when solutions or solution paths are not obvious (MP1);
- reinforce relationships between numbers (MP2);
- discover that numbers are related to other numbers in more than one way (MP2);
- look for patterns within counting numbers, known and unknown numbers (MP7);
- make use of structure when counting (MP8);
- better understand how number charts work and support thinking (MP5); and
- communicate their strategies to others (MP3).

online resources

All tasks can be downloaded for your use at **resources.corwin.com/ jumpstartroutines/elementary**

What They Should Understand First

The Missing does well to complement *The Count* (Routine 2, page 29). This routine builds on fundamental understanding of counting and counting principles. Students should first show proficiency with all counting principles especially one-to-one correspondence and stable-order. Students should also have some experience with other counting strategies, concepts, or skills, including skip-counts, two-more, 10-more, and even two- and 10-less than a number. In kindergarten, this routine may be better reserved for later in the year.

The modifications show how *The Missing* might be used with three-digit numbers and decimals. Before working with either, students should have understanding of the concepts place value and/or decimals. Moreover, those concepts should be developed with appropriate representations that are connected to the number charts. Essentially, students should understand the charts in relationship to the different concepts or numbers before working missing numbers on a minimally complete chart.

What to Do

1. Identify missing numbers on a blank number chart (*Note: The last slide of the downloadable slide deck provides a blank chart and five red highlight boxes that can be dragged to any point on the number chart.*)

2. Fill in numbers on the chart that can be used for finding the targeted missing numbers (the numbers highlighted by red boxes or similar distinction).

3. Have students find the targeted missing numbers.

4. Have students talk with a partner about how they found missing numbers.

5. Bring the group together to discuss how they found missing numbers. During discussion, investigate various student counting strategies. Questions to ask during discussion include:

   » How did you find (a missing number)?

   » How did some of the known numbers help you find (the missing number)?

   » Did anyone find (the missing number) in a different way?

   » How was your strategy similar or different than her strategy?

   » Does your strategy for counting always work?

   » Are there other ways to count that would be more efficient?

   » Why was counting on by ones the best strategy for finding this number?

   » How did you use tens to help you find a number that wasn't just 10 more?

6. Note that students may rely on lower-level, less-complex strategies. In these cases, inject a new strategy (such as counting on from the last known or counting on by tens) as necessary.

7. Consider asking students to find one or two new unknowns on the same chart after students have shared solutions and strategies.

Anticipated Strategies for This Example

1	2	3	4	5	6	7	8		
						17			
	▨								
31									
			54	▨		▨			
61									
						▨			80
									90
▨				95					

For this example, students are asked to find five unknowns. Much of the first row is provided to reinforce how the chart is organized. This is important because later examples will use charts organized in different ways. Your students may find the highlighted missing numbers by counting on from one even though other *knowns* are provided. Some may count on from 8 as it is the last known number in the opening sequence. Other students might skip-count by tens from the opening sequence. For example, they might find 58 by starting with 8 in the top row and counting on by tens. Students might count on by ones from other known numbers finding 55 or 91 in that way. They might count on by ones finding numbers that are farther away such as finding 58 using the last known of 54. Of course, other strategies such as counting back (for finding 78 from 80) might be used. With exposure, students will begin to mix strategies for better efficiencies. In this example, students might find 22 by finding one more than 31 and then thinking about 10 less.

THE MISSING—ADDITIONAL EXAMPLES

A. *The Missing* is a ripe opportunity for exploring number relationships and counting strategies. For some students, providing minimal knowns might be problematic at first. Example A shows how you might modify the chart to provide a few more anchors for students to use. The example offers some things to keep in mind when selecting numbers to use. First and foremost, even with additional numbers offered there are still a considerable number of missing numbers so that students are at least exposed to strategies beyond counting on from one. Another thing to keep in mind is the intentionality of the provided numbers. For example, anchors of 10 more and 10 less are offered for finding 82 but 81 and 83 are not offered.

A

1	2	3	4	5	6	7	8	9	10
11	12			15					
	▨	23				27	28	29	30
						37			
	▨					57			
					▨				
71	72	73				77			▨
	▨					87			
91	92	93				97			

B. Students will show preference for certain strategies with most every skill or concept in mathematics. Strategies may be comfortable but inefficient. You can adjust the routine and prompts to nudge your students to practice more efficient strategies. The charts you use in *The Missing* can support that as well. A different decade is offered as an anchor support in Example B. One and 100 are still provided to help students understand the orientation and organization of the chart. However, students have to take advantage of 10 more and 10 less to find highlighted unknowns on this chart.

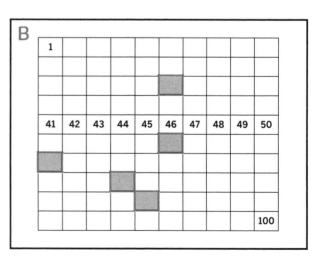

C. Students who find missing numbers on a number chart may not possess advanced counting strategies. Their success may be attributed to continuously counting on from one each time. Others are successful but are unable to make sense of *why* a number is placed where it is. For them, the idea of numbers getting *bigger* as they go down the chart is difficult to reconcile. Other successful students see patterns visually but not mathematically. In other words, they see the tens place change by one digit in each new row but don't recognize that it is 10 more or 10 less than the adjacent row. They don't truly understand counting, skip-counting, patterns, relationships, and number representations on a number chart. To expose possible misunderstanding and more importantly to develop and refine understanding, you can change the orientation of the number chart as done in Example C (Bay-Williams & Fletcher, 2017). Here, the number chart counts left to right and places 1 on the bottom left of the chart. The entire first row is provided to help students understand orientation and organization of the chart.

C

				95	96	97	98	99	100
						87			
71	▓					▓			80
						67	68	69	70
					▓			▓	60
41					46			49	50
									40
▓				25					30
				15					
1	2	3	4	5	6	7	8	9	10

D. There are other ways to manipulate number charts. In Example D, a chart has been arranged to count by ones starting in the upper left-hand corner. Successive numbers are below one another with each new 10 creating a new column. This chart may seem like the most challenging chart, but it may only be so because it is the least familiar if recognizable at all. Yet, after taking a moment to make sense of it one can find that it is just as easy to use as the traditional number chart. You might argue that using this chart or even that of Example E will confuse your students. That may be so. And if true, it likely confuses them because they don't fully understand counting and number relationships. This strengthens the argument for modifying charts and using diverse tools to develop students' understanding. Even so, keep in mind that it might make most sense to develop skills and concepts with one chart before asking students to transfer understanding to other versions of number charts.

D

1	11		31			61			
2									
3	▓	23							93
4		24							
5	15	25	35	45	55	65	75	85	95
6				▓			▓		
7									
8							▓		
9									99
▓	20	30	40	50	60	70	80	90	100

THE MISSING VARIATION—DIFFERENT NUMBER RANGES

You might find that your students continue to rely on certain strategies for finding unknown numbers in this routine. Their preferred strategy is likely counting on or back by ones. You can modify the anchor numbers so that using tens and other strategies become more efficient. You can adjust the routine to help students transfer counting strategies to different number ranges as well as make connections between numbers of three- and possibly four-digits.

E. Number charts that are used with kindergarten and first grade students work well to help them become familiar with patterns and relationships. Older students would benefit from using recognizable charts to build capacity with semi-related numbers. In other words, they might be able to make connections and achieve proficiency sooner if they were to work with charts that had similar design. Example E offers that possibility for the routine. Here, the number chart is a 100 chart that features numbers between 301 and 400. You could adjust charts to represent any collection of 100 numbers possibly even more. You could modify the chart to show 401 to 500, 501 to 600, and so on. You might even change the chart so that it begins with a number like 751 and ends with 850. This latter example still makes use of one hundred however it *bridges a century* as it would include the sequence of 798, 799, 800, 801, and 802. With any of these charts, you should listen for students who transfer ideas of counting from one chart to another by generalizing what it means to count and while almost ignoring the specified 100 for a moment. Other students may revert to earlier counting strategies as newer, greater numbers are offered thus counting on from the beginning number all over again.

E

301	302	303	304	305					310
311	312								
341	342				346	347			350
									360
			384			387	388	389	390
		393							

F. Example F shows another way in which you might alter a number chart for this routine. In fact, it shows two. The first is a 30 chart and the second is a 50 chart. Both charts are likely best used for introducing new limits or extents of counting numbers. A smaller chart, such as a 20 chart, might be better suited for kindergartners. In any of these cases, you can arrange these charts in different ways as explained in Examples C and D. You should note that Example F shows two different charts to give a sense of how you can modify the routine rather than insinuate that you should use two different charts at the same time – though this could be an option in some classrooms.

F

1	2	3	4	5				9	10
11	12	13					18	19	
			24	25	26	27	28	29	30

1		3			6		8	9	10
		13	14	15		17		19	20
	22	23	24	25		27	28	29	30
31	32		34	35					
41	42	43	44	45	46	47	48	49	50

THE MISSING VARIATION—DECIMAL CHARTS

Traditional 100 charts record the 100 whole numbers between two whole numbers. With this understanding, charts can be altered to work with any two numbers separated by a 100 regardless of place value. So, the 100 chart can easily become a decimal chart as there are 100 hundredths between 0 and 1 or 100 thousandths between 0 and $\frac{1}{10}$

G. For many students, early understanding of decimals is relegated to connecting tenths and hundredths to money. And for a subset of these students, their understanding of decimals will be limited to that without specific development. This occurs when students are never helped to see the relationship between place values or the connections with ideas about whole numbers. Leveraging a decimal chart in *The Missing* can alleviate some of this concern.

Example G shows what this might look like. Here, students are prompted to find .22, .55, .58, .78, and .91 by counting on or backwards by hundredths or tenths. This example has the same highlighted unknowns as the featured example for this routine. With this in mind, some students or classes will benefit from using a related whole number 100 chart beside the decimal chart so that they can make connections and refine their understanding of decimals and counting with decimals.

G

.01	.02	.03	.04	.05	.06	.07	.08	.09	.10
.11	�								
				.25					
				.35					
									.50
.51	.52			▒			▒		.60
			.74				▒		
								.89	.90
▒								.99	1.00

H. Expanding work with decimals from hundredths to thousandths is a very difficult transition for many teachers and students. For one, human brains are challenged to make sense of numbers as the numbers get increasingly larger or smaller (Krasa & Shunkwiler, 2009). Other challenges lie in the tools and representations used to develop understanding. The problem with transitioning to thousandths is that money can no longer be used effectively. Base 10 blocks and other models, including grids, offer hope. Fortunately, there are one hundred thousandths between 0 and one tenth. To reflect this, you can modify the decimal chart once again. Example H shows how the chart can be used to represent thousandths so that upper elementary students can develop counting skills with more complex numbers.

H

.001	.002	.003	.004	.005	.006	.007	.008	.009	.010
.011									.020
	▒			.025					.030
				.035					
									.050
.051	.052			▒			▒		.060
.061									
.071	.072	.073	.074		.076		▒		.080
								.089	.090
▒								.099	.100

BIG OR SMALL (MAGNITUDE)

About the Routine

People manipulate numbers to make arguments. Numbers are sometimes exaggerated to convey how outrageous something is. Young students may exclaim that there were a million people at their birthday party. As adults, we know that a million guests is impossible. For those students, they are simply trying to tell us that a lot of people were at the party. A million is a familiar term that describes a large quantity rather than a specific number. Students know that a million is a big number if not an exact amount. But is it always? What if it were describing the grains of sand on a beach? Would a million still be a big number? What if it was describing the number of gallons of water in a lake or the number of people who went to see a movie in a month? Is a million always a large number? In this routine, *Big or Small*, students are prompted to consider when a number is just that—big or small. It helps students develop meaning and context for numbers. It helps students develop magnitude of number by relating numbers to each other and to those contexts. There are all sorts of ways to make use of this routine. Ideally, numbers and

> 73 and 48
> are BIG numbers
> when

contexts are posed for students to determine if the number is big or small. For some, they may first need to consider specific situations. In other instances, the written situations can be replaced with images. In any case, *Big or Small* is a routine that allows for, if not encourages, silliness and humor. And, that is okay. Math can be fun and entertaining. Numbers can be used to communicate, to convince, or to convey absurdity.

Why It Matters

This routine helps students:

- reason about quantity (MP2);
- determine the magnitude of a number based on context (MP2);
- understand reasonableness of a number or of numbers that can be applied to solutions to problems (MP2);

- think critically about numbers and various possibilities;
- create arguments to justify their thinking (MP3);
- consider the reasonableness of arguments made by others (MP3); and
- enjoy mathematics through play and novelty.

 All tasks can be downloaded for your use at **resources.corwin.com/ jumpstartroutines/elementary**

What They Should Understand First

Big or Small is intended to develop students' sense of quantity. There are no specific skills or concepts that students should work with prior to the routine necessarily. However, your students should show proficiency with counting and place value. Initially, the numbers you use in the routine should align with the numbers or size of numbers that your students have been learning about currently or previously. For example, kindergarten and first grade students should experience numbers through 100 and their first exposures to *Big or Small* might have numbers considerably smaller like 10, 15, or 20 if not single digits. In second grade and parts of third grade, students should work with numbers between 100 and 1,000. Even so, these students and those in later grades, should be prompted to think about smaller numbers (0 to 100) from time to time. Fourth and fifth graders should work with numbers in the thousands, ten thousands, and possibly more. Yet, many of these older students will need to work with much smaller numbers first as they may have a good understanding of place value but their sense of quantity and magnitude may be still developing.

What to Do

1. Identify a number or set of numbers.

2. Ask students to think about and create a situation of when that number would be big or small. (*Note: One number can be considered and discussed at a time if more than one number is posed to students.*)

3. Have students discuss with a partner about situations or contexts when the number might be big or small.

4. Have the group share examples of when the number is big or small. During the discussion, questions to ask include:
   » How did you determine if the number was big or small?
   » How did you think about the (context)?
   » When did you see an example of that (context)?
   » How is your (context) similar to others' ideas?
   » What would be an amount you would expect for that (context)?
   » What would be a big or small number for that (context)? (*Note: With this question you are asking the opposite of the prompt on the slide.*)
   » Are there any ideas that you disagree with?

5. Make a mental note about certain contexts or quantities that are especially challenging for students to consider. Revisit in later versions of the routine. These challenges may be addressed through further exploration and discussion or by finding pictures of the context for discussion at a later time.

6. After discussion of a number, consider asking students to create a new context for the same number to determine if they are able to transfer their thinking.

Anticipated Strategies for This Example

> 73 and 48
> are BIG numbers
> when

For this example, students are asked to consider when 73 and 48 are big numbers. As noted in the directions, they might be asked to think about and discuss 73 before then shifting to 48 if the time allotted for the routine permits. *Big or Small* is a unique routine in that student strategies will be solely related to their experiences and perspectives. The same numbers are likely to yield completely different responses in any two classrooms though holidays, current events, and common interests such as sporting events and entertainment are likely to be cited. In any case, you should be prepared to think about what is reasonable. For the example, 73 is a big number if it is the number of students in your classroom though it is not a big number if it is the number of students in your entire school. 73 is a really big number if it is the number of players on a soccer team. People are used as the context in both of these examples. While acceptable, it might warn you that your students have a limited perspective about number and context. In other words, you should listen for and prompt new and different contexts when necessary. For example, 73 is also a big number if it is the number of dogs a family has as pets. 73 is a big number if it is the number of cookies eaten for dinner. It is a big number if it is the number of cars in someone's driveway.

BIG OR SMALL—ADDITIONAL EXAMPLES

A. *Big or Small* asks students to think about when numbers are big and small. In the featured example, students consider if 73 and 48 are big. The following day you might ask your students if the same numbers are small. Example A shows that. Students might be asked to consider if a number was big or small in the same day or at the same time. But, there might be benefits to separating the ideas and extending them over two days. This allows time for students to reflect on and look for new and different instances when the featured numbers are big. It also allows time for students to process the idea of the number being *big* when students hadn't considered it to be. The next day, you and your class can recount examples of the number being big before you pivot to asking when those same numbers will seem small.

> A
>
> 73 and 48
> are SMALL numbers when

B. It's easy for students to recognize that a thousand is a big number even though it isn't always. Your students may think that a hundred of anything will be a lot. But, *small* numbers can represent ideas about big as well. As students become comfortable with the routine, you can introduce new perspectives about number and magnitude. Example B is one of those examples. For most students, 12 and 8 are not indicative of something big. However, when someone has 12 pieces of pizza for lunch the number is very big. When a student has 8 siblings, 8 becomes very big. Example B is a reminder that students will need opportunities to wrestle with seemingly small numbers that actually represent large quantities.

> B
>
> 12 and 8
> are BIG numbers when

C. Contrary to Example B, *Big or Small* can pose seemingly large numbers masquerading as something quite small. Example C shows what that might look like. At first, this might be quite challenging for students. However, you can share examples that help your students make sense of the *big* number and the context. Discussion and exposure to new ideas can help students expand their thinking about these numbers. 580 does seem like a big number until it's thought of as the number of people in an NFL stadium, the number of people that live in a city, or the number of feet someone runs when jogging. Even 2,000 is small if it is the number of pages in all of the books on a book shelf, if it is the number of seconds for a trip, or the number of page views for a certain website.

> **C**
>
> 580 and 2,000
> are SMALL numbers when

D. It's likely that many students have never considered a number to be big or small. To them, certain numbers are big and others are small irrelevant of context. For them, the opening examples of this routine might be problematic. Instead, you might have to give them specific examples to think about in order to develop their ideas about any number being both big and small. Example D shows what this looks like. Here, students determine if 73 is big or small if it is the number of cupcakes to be eaten, if it is the number of dogs someone has, or if it is the number of people in a movie theater. This version of *Big or Small* might be the best place to start because the contexts are familiar and provided. It could also be used to help students write their own big and small situations that you could use in a later offering of the routine.

> **D**
>
> **73 is BIG or SMALL when describing the**
>
> - number of cupcakes
> - number of dogs
> - number of people at a movie

NOTES

_____

_____

_____

_____

_____

_____

_____

BIG OR SMALL VARIATION—OPEN POSSIBILITIES

The first few examples of *Big or Small* asked students to create situations in which a given number was big or small. The latter examples provide numbers and contexts and students determine if it is representative of big or small. But, what if a possibility was both big and small based on a slightly different context? Students should be able to think critically and make arguments about how something changes as the condition changes.

E. Example E is an example of a variation on the routine that has students think about when a condition could be both big and small. 73 crayons is a big number if it is the number of crayons in a student's pencil box. However, it is also small if it is the number of crayons in the art teacher's class bin or if it is the number of crayons in an entire third grade classroom. Essentially, the number and the thing is both big and small as other information is manipulated. In this example, students would have opportunities to think about both big and small for a given prompt before discussing their ideas with a classmate and eventually sharing out with the class.

E

73 crayons

16 movies

F. Example F shows another example of number contexts that can be both big and small. 100 pennies is a lot for a pocket. But, 100 pennies are only one dollar, which isn't a lot of money. Similarly, 500 lightbulbs would be a big number if it was the number of lightbulbs in someone's house. Of course, it is a small number if it is the number of lights used to decorate that house for a holiday celebration. *Big or Small* affords you the opportunity to keep a routine, or a mathematics discussion, going throughout the day or week. You might record student ideas about a certain number and context on a chart or poster paper displayed in the classroom or on a bulletin board. Throughout the day or week, students could add new examples of when the number is big or small. This serves many purposes. Most notably, it strengthens student understanding and perspective of number and magnitude by positioning them to continuously look for and think about situations in which numbers are either big or small.

F

100 pennies

500 lightbulbs

BIG OR SMALL VARIATION—FRACTIONS

The idea of a whole number being large or small is likely more natural or intuitive for students. Students are usually more comfortable with whole numbers. This may be one of the reasons that students are challenged to reason and compute with other types of numbers, including fractions and decimals. *Big or Small* has the potential to help those upper elementary students.

G. Thinking about fractions as being big or small will be a bit different for students at first. It will likely remain challenging until students begin to think about fractions in the same ways that they think about whole numbers. It may also be challenging for you to think about contexts and situations for fractions to pose to students. When you first work with fractions in this routine, it might be most conducive for you to give a fraction and a context for students to consider. This approach is similar to that in Example D with a similar rationale. Example D notes that students may have never considered a (whole) number to be big or small. It is even more likely that they have never thought of a fraction as being big or small. Students are asked to determine if $\frac{3}{4}$ of a pound is big or small. It might be both. It is really small if it is listed as the weight of a laptop. Yet, $\frac{3}{4}$ of a pound is a lot of fudge to eat for a snack. As with whole numbers, the magnitude of fractions changes as the context or situation in which they refer to are changed.

H. Using fractions instead of whole numbers presents an interesting slant on this routine. However, the basic construct remains the same. You can give your students a fraction and ask them to think about when it is big or small (Examples A and B). You can give a list of situations for a specific fraction and ask students to consider if each line item is big or small (Examples D and G). In other cases, you can give a fraction and ask students to create a situation in which it is big or small. Example H prompts students to think about when a fraction $\left(\frac{1}{2}\right)$ is both big and small. This example and all others can make use of any fraction. You can easily change the prompt to use $\frac{1}{3}, \frac{4}{5}$, or even $3\frac{3}{4}$ as mixed numbers offer a whole new slew of possibilities. As noted previously, students can be asked to create numbers and situations that teachers can use in the routine. They might do this during independent work or for homework. You might also work together with colleagues to create and share examples to lessen your workload.

> **G**
>
> Is $\frac{3}{4}$ BIG or SMALL?
>
> - number of pounds
> - number of miles
> - of a cookie

> **H**
>
> $\frac{1}{2}$ is a BIG number when it is _____
>
> $\frac{1}{2}$ is a SMALL number when it is _____.

PICTURE IT (MAGNITUDE AND ESTIMATION)

About the Routine

Numbers are everywhere. They are much more than the problems on a page. We use them to describe the world, to solve problems, and to ask questions about the world. Often, we make assumptions and decisions based on observation and quantitative reasoning. For example, we might choose a certain checkout line at a store because there appear to be fewer people in it. In other cases, we might choose a line with more people because the line with fewer people has more items to be scanned. We might look at a gymnasium and consider it half full. We might select a certain cookie because it appears to have more chocolate chips. Mathematicians determine the number of people at an inauguration or the number of people at a parade by estimating and modeling with mathematics. They quantify a sample and apply it to the larger image or situation. This routine, *Picture It,* is designed to unlock students' interest and wonder about the mathematics around them. They are asked to analyze possibilities in a picture. In some cases, they are asked to reason about a total number or to compare numbers. In other cases, they are asked to make observations, estimates, or to determine how they might count something in the picture. It

How many are there altogether?

can empower students to reason without concern of being *wrong*. Students are presented with a picture and asked to simply look for mathematics within the picture. Teachers then pose questions for them to consider and discuss with a partner. The class then talks about possible solutions and more importantly the reasoning applied to those solutions. In the building block picture, we might ask "How many blocks are?", "How many nubs are there in the entire creation?", or "How many blocks would there be if it was made twice as large?"

Why It Matters

This routine helps students:

- look for mathematics in their environment;
- apply mathematics concepts to real-world situations;
- pursue solutions with no clear solution path (MP1);

All tasks can be downloaded for your use at **resources.corwin.com/jumpstartroutines/elementary**

- reason about number and quantity in the real world (MP2);
- model with mathematical ideas to solve problems (MP4);

- refine strategies and ideas about estimation (MP2); and
- communicate their reasoning to others (MP3).

What They Should Understand First

Picture It always works regardless of your students' grade level or mathematics proficiency. Its complexity and rigor are tied directly to the questions we ask about the pictures. It is a flexible routine that can be applied to any picture or any mathematics concept. It may be best used simply to promote estimation, reasoning, and problem solving. Students do not need specific content skills to engage with *Picture It*. Instead, they need other less tangible skills. For many, it may be one of their first opportunities to observe and think about open-ended applications of mathematics.

They may be challenged to think about the mathematics in a picture. Your questions are an opportunity for problem solving. Students will need to be comfortable with situations that have no specific entry point or solution pathway. They should have some ideas about estimation, but there is no minimal level of proficiency needed. Their estimation will improve through exposure to this and other routines. They should also have a mindset of perseverance and various possibilities and approaches to solve a problem.

What to Do

1. Select a picture and create a question to ask about the picture.

2. Display the picture and give students a few moments to examine it.

3. Pose the question to students. An example for the building block picture could be "How many nubs are there altogether in the structure?"

4. Give students time to think about an answer to the question. Consider allowing students to capture some thoughts on sticky notes, whiteboards, or index cards.

5. Have students share their solutions and reasoning with a partner.

6. Bring the class back together to share solutions.

7. After collecting three or four solutions, ask students to share their reasoning.

8. Highlight student ideas during discussion. Questions to ask (for the question above) might include:

   » How did you find the total nubs in the structure?

   » How did you think about the picture?

   » Are there any unknowns that you can't answer from the picture?

   » What assumptions did you have to make? Why?

   » How did you reason about the total number of blocks?

   » What is a reasonable number of blocks in the structure?

   » How did you count the nubs in the picture?

   » What would be a completely unreasonable solution? Why?

9. Honor and explore all reasoning. Be sure to counter both logical and flawed reasoning with questions rather than confirmations of *right* or *wrong*.

10. Consider asking students to think of other questions that they can ask about the picture. These questions might be used in subsequent classes.

Anticipated Strategies for This Example

For the building blocks picture, the question posed was "How many nubs are there altogether in the structure?" Your students might consider only the nubs they can see. They'll offer 24 or something close. You can ask them about how they counted the total. Some will share that they counted by ones, others by twos, some by fours, and possibly some by sixes. Some students will show how they found and made use of 10. Some students will disagree with 24 arguing that there are nubs on the bottom row of blocks, too. These students will suggest that there are 48.

Strategies for finding this total will likely include ideas about finding the top layer and doubling with addition. Some may count each visible nub twice to compensate for the hidden nubs below. These students should be asked about how they found the number of blocks in the bottom layer or if the bottom layer matters. You should give students a chance to argue about assumptions they made as well as how the number of individual blocks on the bottom row doesn't matter so long as the general structure is the same. It's possible that some students will make claims that the bottom row isn't complete or that the middle is also filled in. These ideas should be accepted so long as their reasoning and count are compatible.

PICTURE IT—ADDITIONAL EXAMPLES

A. A good place to begin with *Picture It* is for you to simply pose a picture to students and to ask them what they notice about it. This approach works in any grade. It is useful because it will help students develop observational skills and quantitative reasoning about images and contexts that can be applied to other versions of the routine. Here, in Example A, students might notice that there are 12 donuts. Some might notice that there are three chocolate frosted donuts. They might notice that there are three heart-shaped donuts or that six donuts have a *hole* in the middle. You can prompt students to share how they counted the donuts. You can draw attention to the structure, shape, or organization of the picture and how those help students count. You might even suggest that counting by other numbers, such as two, can be faster. This can be introduced even if students haven't learned about skip-counting. In time, you can record equations to describe pictures or you can ask students to write equations themselves to make numerical notes about the images.

A

What do you notice about the picture?

B. You can provide benchmarks in pictures for students to use in order to find totals or other amounts. In Example B, you tell students how many windows are on the two visible sides of a building. With that information, you ask students how many windows are on the whole building. Even with the given, students still have to make assumptions about the building. Students might find the amount of one side and double it before doing the same for the other sides. Other students might consider one *level* or *floor* of windows (both sides) to have 20 as there are 10 visible in a level and so they can double that amount. Your discussion doesn't have to be about what is *easiest* or most efficient. Instead, you can use it to simply help students see diverse pathways for finding solutions. Also, note that there are two windows on the ground floor which may go unnoticed by some.

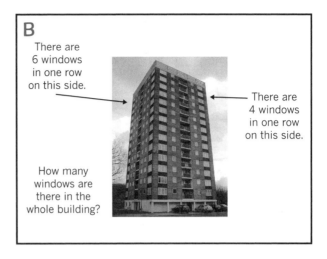

B

There are 6 windows in one row on this side.

There are 4 windows in one row on this side.

How many windows are there in the whole building?

C. Like other routines, *Picture It* is a wonderful opportunity for you to develop estimation skills. Example C shows how you might prompt estimations through the routine. Here, you can ask students about how many cookies there are. You should be on the lookout for students who count and then offer an estimate. Instead, students should make estimates and then count the picture to determine if estimates were reasonable. Beginning with this version is important as it helps students practice making estimates and comparing to knowns or actual amounts. Students who estimate first and then compare to actuals improve precision and reasonableness of estimates over time.

C

About how many cookies are there?

D. Having your students notice patterns and quantities in images and the world around them, as noted in Example A, is invaluable. Prompting your students to ask questions is equally important. It helps them think about possibilities while also considering how questions are asked and problems are posed. You can expect students to first ask questions unrelated to math. When your students do this, you can simply redirect them to think about the picture mathematically. You could also accept a *non-math* question and then counter with a math question. Or, you could accept a *non-math* question before you redirect the group to reconsider the image mathematically. In this example, your students might ask about the number of horses, eyes, tails, or legs. They might ask about weight and length. They might even ask questions about the height of a horse or the fence. From time to time, student questions are likely to surprise you. In fact, you can collect questions to investigate in subsequent lessons.

D

What question do you have about the picture?

NOTES

_____

_____

_____

_____

_____

_____

_____

_____

_____

_____

_____

_____

_____

PICTURE IT VARIATION—COUNT AND COMPARE

Students—even older ones—can continue to find discussions about how to count groups of objects challenging. You can amplify counting strategies, estimation, and magnitude if you ask students to consider how a quantity relates to a given value before finding the amount.

E. Are there more or less than 10 cookies in the picture? Are there more or less than 20, 50, or even 100? You might pose these questions in Example B. Then, you can ask students to think about why their estimates are reasonable and how they determined their estimates. After that discussion, you can ask students to count items in the picture individually and to share their strategies with a partner or the group. During this discussion, students are exposed to strategies that challenge their thinking of process and efficiency. In the picture, students might count the column of cookies from left to right before counting those on top. Some might count from the top first or from the right first. Students might suggest counting by ones or twos depending on their grade level.

F. Of course, counting becomes more complicated as more and more objects need to be counted. As with Example E, you can first ask students if there are more or less than 10, 20, or 50 birds in the picture. Then, you can ask students to count the number of birds. Some may count all of the birds on each wire. Some students might count one wire and attempt to double amount showing that exacts aren't always needed for confirming that estimates are reasonable. Some students might share that they found the amount of space 10 birds take and then found the number of those spaces in the picture.

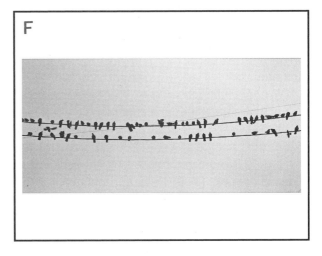

PICTURE IT VARIATION—ESTIMATES WITHOUT ACTUALS

Students' estimation experiences should be grounded in work in which estimates can be confirmed by finding exacts such as Example C. Yet, in the real-world estimates are made without being able to confirm reasonableness with counting. Instead, people rely on reasoning and number sense developed by experience and opportunity.

G. What is a good estimate for the number of cookies in the picture? What is a bad estimate? How do you know? These are all good questions to pose for Example G. Here, students are asked to estimate the number of cookies without being able to find the exact amount. Students might be challenged to think about how many cookies are hidden in the pile. So, early work with these versions of the routine may need to be buoyed by your reasoning. Students' attention might be directed to the size of one or two cookies or the height of three or four cookies. Armed with this thinking, students can then project how many are on the entire plate. You should also consider prompting students to think about and justify what is a reasonable or unreasonable number of cookies *hidden* in the picture.

G

About how many cookies are on the plate?

H. About how many cargo containers are on the ship? Are there about 5, 10, or 20? Are there more or less than 50? These questions work well with Example H. It is another example of the routine in which students are asked to estimate but won't be able to find an actual answer. However, students are able to determine the size of one container and apply that to the size of the stacks and the attributes of the boat. Students may be able to see a three-by-four-by-three stack of containers in the *middle* of the ship. Students might think about how the length of a container compares to its width to determine if any are stacked perpendicular to the those running parallel to the ship's length.

H

About how many containers are on the ship?

The picture also offers another idea about how a benchmark can be applied to an estimation. Instead of asking about the number of containers, you might ask fourth or fifth graders to think about how many feet tall one of the stacks might be. At first, this might seem impossible. But there are benchmarks in the picture. If you look closely you see that there is a person on the right side of the boat. People are about five or six feet tall. You can use that person to determine the height of the stack or possibly the length of the boat. Even if you missed the person, you cannot overlook the doors. You could use the height of the doors as a benchmark in the exact same way.

SHOW IT 3 (REPRESENTING NUMBERS)

About the Routine

Take a moment to think about how you and your students represent numbers or concepts in class. How would you represent 6×4, $\frac{3}{4}$, or the number 37? Would you use an array, area model, repeated addition, a comparison model, or something else for 6×4? Would you use number lines, pattern blocks, fraction tiles, circles, or something else for $\frac{3}{4}$? Do you think 37 best shown with base 10 blocks, 10 frames, a number line, or a 100 chart? Each of us has a preference for the representations we use to communicate meaning and understanding. Our preference may even become a bias as we use one representation predominantly over time in our classroom. The predominance of one representation instead of another can be problematic for students. It might even limit the extent to which they understand a concept. Instead, students should have opportunities to work with all sorts of representations and see connections between them. They should think about and represent concepts with words, models, pictures, symbols, and contexts (Lesh, Post, & Behr, 1987). In this routine, students are asked

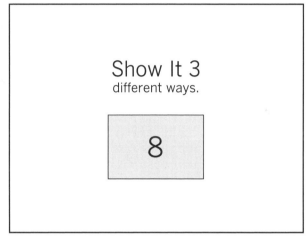

Show It 3
different ways.

8

to represent numbers in three different ways. Like other routines, it can be done as an opening activity on the carpet or floor area. However, you might also consider having students at small group tables or something similar so that they can access physical tools if they choose. Once settled, students are prompted to represent a given number in three different ways. They share their ideas with partners or their small group before you solicit diverse examples from the class.

Why It Matters

This routine helps students:

- think strategically about numbers and open problems (MP1);

- identify new representations for a number;

- make sense of how tools and models represent a number (MP4);

 All tasks can be downloaded for your use at **resources.corwin.com/ jumpstartroutines/elementary**

- reinforce their perception of the meaning of a number (MP2);
- make connections between representations and tools (MP2);
- determine advantages and disadvantages of different tools and representations (MP5);
- leverage representations to communicate their understanding (MP3);
- recognize others' perspectives and ideas about number (MP3); and
- see structure within representations as new numbers are presented (MP7).

What They Should Understand First

Show It 3 intends to reinforce students' ideas about how to represent numbers. Students should understand the number or number concept inherent in the prompt. They should learn about diverse representations before practicing them through the routine. For this example (show 8 three different ways), students might use a 10 frame, counters, and a number chart. To do so, they must understand how each of these tools and/or representations work. Students should understand that 10 frames are frames for counters that can be placed anywhere in the frame. They can organize counters in certain ways to make counting easier but there are no explicit rules for working with 10 frames. Students should be comfortable with other representations like number lines or number paths so that they can use them in the routine. In this example, students must understand ideas about counting and quantity so they might use any collection of counters, including buttons, blocks, beans, or even paper clips. As students work with multi-digit numbers, understanding of place value will be essential for successfully representing numbers.

What to Do

1. Consider how students will be directed to represent the number. Will they be asked to use physical tools? If so, be sure to distribute physical tools (counters, magnetic frames, blocks, dominos, etc.) prior to the routine. You can also direct them to lapboards or journals to draw the representations.

2. Pose the number and have students represent the number in three different ways.

3. Have students share their representations with a partner before sharing examples as a class. (Note: *Gallery walk*, where students visit others' work, would be a good alternative if students made models at their tables.)

4. Record examples of student representations.

5. Discuss class representations during or after recording ideas. Questions to ask might include:

   » How are the representations different?
   » How are the representations connected?
   » Which representation do you prefer?
   » Which representation was hardest for you to think about?
   » Is there a representation that surprised you? Why?
   » How would the representation for (number) change if we changed it to (different number)?

6. Consider inserting a representation that was overlooked or not shared. Discuss this representation if needed.

7. If necessary, introduce or reinforce drawings that represent physical tools students use (e.g., sticks and dots for base 10 blocks).

Anticipated Strategies for This Example

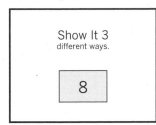

This example, show 8 in three different ways, is intended for a kindergarten classroom. Students should understand counting principles about number, counting, and quantity. They are likely to use representations that you have featured during instruction. They might arrange eight counters in a *line* of eight. Some might arrange them in a circle or in some other grouping. It's also possible that students might use counters for all three representations simply arranging them in different ways as noted (line, group, circle, etc.). You should acknowledge them and take note. It will serve as a good discussion point with the class later in the routine. Students might fill a row in a 10 frame and have three in the other row. However, some students might put four in one row and four in another. Students might select a domino from a pile that represents 8. In the case of dominoes, it would be interesting for you to see if students select only one example of 8 or more than one. Even those who select more than one might not select all of the eights from the pile. Their selections may tell you about their understanding or comfort with a number and number representations or combinations.

SHOW IT 3—ADDITIONAL EXAMPLES

A. *Show It 3* works well in any mathematics class. You can easily adjust the routine to fortify understanding of more complex numbers. Example A presents a two-digit number that might be used in first or early second grade. Students could represent this number with base 10 models, including base 10 blocks, Digi-blocks®, or 10 frames. They might represent two-digit numbers, number bonds, or they might identify the location of these numbers on a 100 chart or number line. Essentially, these multi-digit numbers have a host of possibilities much like any number. And, your students should be adept in representing and connecting representations of these numbers.

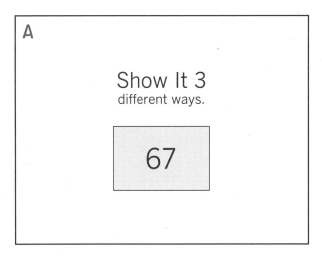

B. As students work with representations, they make connections and recognize patterns. This can lead to misconceptions about how the tool or representation works. It's possible that students recognize a certain image as a number more so than what the quantity that the representation means. In other words, these students might only see 27 with two tens followed by seven ones. They might know it to be 27 if it was a 10, five ones, another 10, and then two ones. You can advance their understanding by prompting them to show a number in three different ways with the same tool. As in Example B, students might be asked to show 37 in three different ways with base 10 blocks or sticks and dots. They might show it with three sticks and seven dots, followed by two sticks, seven dots, and one more stick. A third showing might be five dots, three sticks, and two more dots. It's also possible that some students only *see* 37 as three sticks to the left of seven dots.

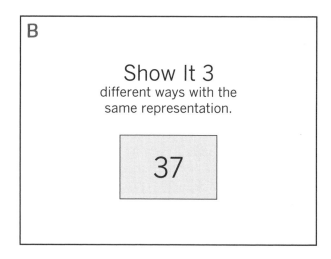

C. Tools and representations show tremendous value as students learn about operations (Van de Walle et al., 2019). You can use *Show It 3* to help students build a deeper understanding of operations as shown in Example C. As with other examples, students might use physical models or drawings of those models to show the computation. Here, they might show 5 + 8 on a double 10 frame. They might show it with counters or blocks. Some might make use of a number line. It's also possible that students use decompositions or related facts to represent the expression. For example, they might show 5 + 8 as 3 + 2 + 8 or 3 + 10. The routine shows its greatest potential when these *unexpected* returns come in. You should have the group consider, discuss, and explore. You can expose more complex ideas about facts and computation while connecting to and possibly leveraging rudimentary representations (ten frames, etc.) to justify these complex ideas. The routine can become the catalyst for moving all students—regardless of their starting points—forward.

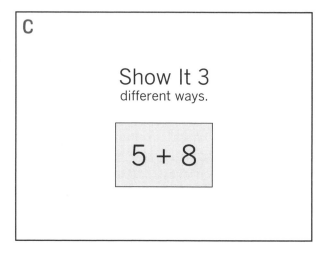

D. Putting together, adding up, or building on may inadvertently dominate games, activities, or routines. Having many games for addition may do well to enhance capacity with the operation. But, it may explain why students are seemingly *better* with addition than subtraction. You can adjust this routine for students to represent subtraction in different ways. Example D prompts students to show 31 – 29 in three different ways. Again, base 10 models, number charts, and number line diagrams are likely to appear. This is good. In time, you can also begin to insert representations of strategies to help students develop flexibility and efficiency. 31 – 29 isn't an attractive choice for strategy exposure and discussion. But if it was 61 – 29, strategy representations to consider might include 62 – 30 (adjusting), 61 – 20 – 9 (partial differences), or 61 – 30 + 1 (compensation).

D

Show It 3
different ways.

31 – 29

NOTES

SHOW IT 3 VARIATION—FRACTIONS

Show It 3 is a routine for building foundations of number. You can modify it like other routines to work with small numbers, multi-digit numbers, fractions, and decimals. It is also important to use this routine with fractions as representational bias mentioned previously also occurs with fractions. Some students perceive fractions as only shaded parts and round foods. Others consistently use the same tool and see the same images repeatedly resulting in skewed ideas that $\frac{1}{3}$ always looks like a *peace sign* and that $\frac{1}{4}$ always looks like a *window pane*.

E. Example E prompts students to represent $\frac{3}{4}$ in three different ways. You can group students and provide them with collections of manipulatives for them to represent the fraction. Students might have access to pattern blocks, color tiles, fraction strips, fraction circles, fraction blocks, Cuisenaire rods, counters, and number lines. For this example, students would choose three of the tools to show $\frac{3}{4}$. The class would then share their representations. During the debriefing discussion, it is critical to discuss how each representation shows $\frac{3}{4}$. In fact, there might be nice opportunities to connect with other concepts such as equivalent fractions. Imagine if a group of students shows $\frac{3}{4}$ with one blue color tile and three red tiles whereas another group shows $\frac{3}{4}$ with two blue tiles and six red tiles. Both groups accurately show $\frac{3}{4}$ but their representations offer much more to talk about.

E

Show It 3
different ways.

$$\frac{3}{4}$$

F. Example F poses the importance of using mixed numbers in routines. Here, students are asked to represent $2\frac{2}{3}$. Again, pattern blocks, Cuisenaire rods, and other tools can be used to show it. You must be on the lookout for the representations that students use most frequently when working with mixed numbers as well. You can use preferred or familiar representations to introduce new concepts like equivalency or computation with fractions. You can also use them to help students better understand a different tool or representation. Keep in mind that preference of a representation or tool might indicate limited understanding of a concept in general.

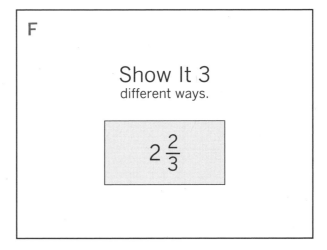

F

Show It 3
different ways.

$$2\frac{2}{3}$$

SHOW IT 3 VARIATION—GEOMETRY

Jump-start routines are intended to develop number sense through brief engagements over long periods of time. They lean toward number concepts. But, these routines work with other concepts from time to time. Like *Math Yapper* (Routine 1, page 22), *Show It 3* can work well with geometry.

G. Understanding is all about perspective. Occasionally, flawed understanding makes perfect sense to students. This quirk can appear as students learn about shapes. For some students, triangles look like a specific thing—usually an equilateral triangle with a wide base narrowing to a point at the *top*. Because of this, they don't see right triangles as triangles. To these students, oddly formed and oriented scalene triangles cannot be triangles either. *Show It 3* is an opportunity for you to help students discover that triangles come in all sorts of shapes, sizes, and orientations. You can feature other geometric concepts, including three-dimensional figures, polygons, non-polygons, types of quadrilaterals, and so on. Tools for the geometry version of this routine are useful as well. You might provide geoboards, pattern blocks, attribute blocks, toothpicks, popsicle sticks, or AngLegs®.

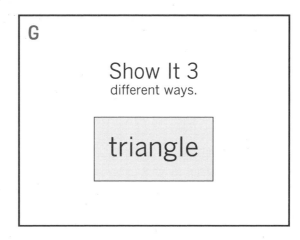

H. Students distort other ideas about geometry as well. They often do this with angles. This happens when they consistently see angles with one horizontal ray and the angle opening on the right. They can then struggle to identify examples of acute angles that *point* down or to the left. These angles may be thought of as obtuse though they are nothing of the sort. Example H shows how you might present angles in this routine. Here an image of an acute angle is presented. Students should then create three different representations or examples of acute angles. You should look for three different angle measures and different orientations in your students' samples. You might find that each angle has the distinct horizontal feature mentioned above. You can present other geometric concepts in the same visual way. Instead of the word triangle (Example G), you could project an image of a triangle to investigate how students *see* concepts.

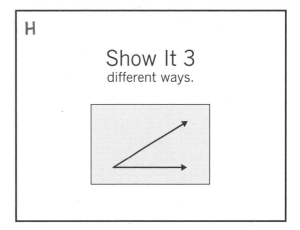

HOW CAN YOU MAKE IT? (DECOMPOSITION)

About the Routine

Decomposition of number is essential for mathematics success. Skilled decomposers are better positioned to be efficient and flexible computers. These students are able to quickly recognize that 64 + 48 is the same as 100 + 12. They are also able to see that 47 + 29 is the same as 50 + 26. They apply understanding to other operations. They are able to think about 181 – 153 as 181 – 150 – 3 or even as 179 – 151. In time, they apply their understanding to partial product and partial quotient strategies. Unfortunately, some students only work with or become proficient with decomposing numbers by their place values. These students only see 83 as 80 and 3. This is a great start, but 83 is much more. 83 might be thought of as 75 and 8, which is helpful for adding 83 + 125. It might be thought of as 79 and 4, 50 and 33, and so on. We develop decomposition and flexible thinking about numbers through instruction, diverse experiences, and opportunities to practice and discuss. In this routine, *How Can You Make It?*, students consider the many ways

to express a number. Students are prompted with a number to decompose. They think about one way to break it apart and share their ideas with a partner. The class shares with the teacher who records the different ideas. After ideas have been shared, you can prompt them to think of a new way to decompose the number that hasn't been shared and recorded already.

> How can you make
>
> **15**?

Why It Matters

This routine helps students:

- consider how to decompose a number (MP2);
- look for patterns and structure within decompositions (MP7);
- manipulate patterns, relationships, and operations (MP8);
- reinforce ideas about friendly numbers or benchmarks (MP2);

- practice computation to improve precision (MP6);
- reflect on diverse approaches to represent a number to determine which are most useful;
- develop confidence with quantity and computation; and
- communicate their reasoning with others (MP3).

 All tasks can be downloaded for your use at **resources.corwin.com/ jumpstartroutines/elementary**

What They Should Understand First

How Do You Make It? works with any number or type of number, including fractions and decimals. You should use it after students show conceptual understanding of number and decomposition. They might show understanding through a collection of representations, but they must also be able to communicate how those representations connect to symbolic representations (numbers). Students should also show some ability to decompose a number. In kindergarten, decomposition might be limited to *one-more than* or *two-more than* a number. For example, they might only be able to think of 11 as 1 and 10 or 2 and 9. In later grades, decomposition might be limited to place value. Either is fine. The routine itself is intended to expose, develop, and reinforce new ideas about decomposing numbers. You might provide students with tools, such as 10 frames or base 10 blocks, during initial exposures to the routine. In these early experiences, you should also record and connect symbolic decompositions to representations if students do not do so themselves.

What to Do

1. Select a number for students to decompose. (Note: Consider giving some examples of how it might be decomposed the first few times the routine is introduced.)

2. Direct students to decompose the number. (Optional: Have students decompose the number in two ways or more than three ways.)

3. Have students share their decomposition(s) with a partner.

4. Have students share their examples with the group.

5. Record student examples. Note that there is no better number of examples to record. In some instances, five will be plenty. In others, nine or 10 examples might be collected and recorded.

6. Discuss with the group the decomposition examples that were recorded. Questions to ask might include:

   » What do you notice about how we decomposed the number?

   » What two decompositions are most alike?

   » How did the numbers in those examples change?

   » Do you notice any patterns in how we broke apart the numbers?

   » Do you think this pattern will work with other numbers?

   » Which of the examples are easiest for you to think about?

   » Which of the examples are hardest for you to think about?

7. After discussion, ask students to decompose the number in a new way that wasn't recorded.

8. Have students share their new decompositions with partners and then the whole class.

Anticipated Strategies for This Example

How can you make
15?

For this example, students are asked to decompose 15. It is a good choice for later in the kindergarten year or early in first grade. Many students are likely to first decompose 15 into 10 and 5. Some students may be able to only decompose it into 10 and 5. Students who extend beyond place value decomposition are likely to use breaking a number into 1 and something and 2 and something. In this example, that would be 14 and 1 and 13 and 2. You should listen for students who consistently share something and 1 or something and 2 for different reasons. Some who rely on a number and 1 (14 and 1) might think of it in ways of counting and may not recognize that it is a decomposition. Those that understand might rely on 1 more and 2 more as their *only* strategies for decomposing. For these and other students it is necessary that you connect those *comfortable decompositions* to different ideas. In this example, 15 decomposed as 14 and 1 or 13 and 2 should be connected 12 and 3, 11 and 4, or anything else. In time, you might pose new challenges to advance student thinking. An example of this might be to decompose 15 with two single-digit numbers to advance student thinking.

HOW CAN YOU MAKE IT? —ADDITIONAL EXAMPLES

A. Ideally, *How Can You Make It?* is a mental mathematics routine. That is, students should not use tools, paper, or lapboards to support their thinking. However, that's not the best place to begin with young students—especially kindergarteners—who are first learning to break apart numbers. Example A shows how you might use this routine with them. Here, 7 is shown on a 10 frame. Students might have personal mini-10 frames with them on the floor to help them manipulate the number. It may be better for students to have a double-10 frame to help them show the number. 7 can be shown as 6 and 1, 5 and 2, or even 3 and 4. You can model the representation (6 + 1, 5 + 2, etc.), record the expression, and connect these as students share their ideas. Young students should not be expected to generate expressions. You can adjust this example of the routine to use groups of counters, counting bears, dot cards, dominos, or blocks.

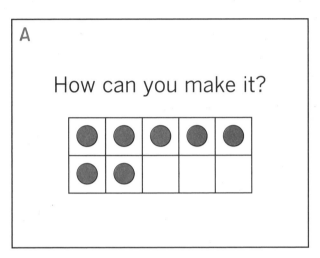

 The Double Ten Frame can be downloaded for your use at
resources.corwin.com/jumpstartroutines/elementary

NOTES

_____

_____

_____

_____

_____

_____

_____

_____

_____

_____

B. Elementary students clearly need to decompose numbers greater than 20. Example B asks students to decompose 84. They might do so by breaking it into 80 and 4, 79 and 5, or something more *exotic* like 60 and 24, 44 and 40, or even 49 and 35. Over time, this should become almost effortless for students. However, some numbers might be problematic at first. It is likely best for them to first work with friendly numbers and benchmarks. So, students might first work to decompose tens such as 30, 40, or 80. Then, students might work with benchmark numbers of 25, 50, or 75 before working with numbers like 84, 71, or 43. As your students' confidence and proficiency grows, you can shift the routine to explore decomposition of these *different* numbers. Using this progression enables students to leverage ideas about friendlies and benchmarks in order to decompose other numbers like 84, 71, and 43.

C. It makes sense to expose students to decomposing three-digit numbers. It is helpful for them to find partial sums and differences on a number line or even mentally. Like other numbers, there is no limit to how three-digit numbers can be decomposed. Again, like other numbers, students are most likely to initially rely on decomposition through place value. If and when this happens, you may need to offer a new example for students to make use of. For 350, you might share 250 and 100 as a possible decomposition as well as other examples. You might decide to place *limitations* or restrictions on how your students can decompose numbers. For this example, you might ask students to decompose 350 into two numbers with one of those numbers being greater than 300. Or, you might ask them to decompose 350 into two numbers that both have more than four ones. Making this adjustment helps students break out of safe decompositions so that you can advance their understanding. It could be used with smaller numbers in earlier grades as well.

B

How can you make

84?

C

How can you make

350?

D. Sometimes, we make inadvertent missteps when we accept the same types or strategies for decomposition. Continuously breaking apart numbers in the same ways become habitual decompositions. Thoughts about 350, shared above, are good examples of this. Students who consistently decompose numbers into place value or one part that has no ones (e.g., 84 as 70 and 14, 60 and 24, or 350 as 340 and 10, 330 and 20) seem to be *fluent* but their understanding may not be very deep. Example D shows how you can adjust this routine to tackle that challenge. It asks students to decompose numbers into more than two parts. Here, students are asked to decompose 15 (the original example) into three numbers. Students might first think about 10, 2, and 3, which is completely fine. From there, students might think about 7, 7, and 1 or something similar. Students in any grade can decompose a number into three parts. You might provide a triple ten frame for young students to organize their thinking when breaking a number into three parts.

> **D**
>
> How can you make
>
> # 15
>
> with **three** numbers?

 A Triple Ten Frame can be downloaded for your use at resources.corwin.com/jumpstartroutines/elementary

NOTES

HOW CAN YOU MAKE IT? VARIATION—BASIC FACTS AND COMPUTATION

Learning to decompose numbers may be most applicable to computation. But while some students are able to decompose numbers when they appear in isolation, they are sometimes unable to translate their understanding of computations. This occurs for a variety of reasons most particularly when they are rushed to learn procedures without having lots of opportunities to explore patterns and relationships that underpin computational strategies. In other cases, students are exposed to these strategies but don't have enough time to discuss and reinforce the connections.

E. You can modify *How Can You Make It?* to make connections between decomposition of number and basic facts. It can galvanize students' acquisition and usage of basic fact strategies. Example E shows what that might look like. Here, students are asked how they can make 6 + 9. Granted some students might be able to simply recall the sum. Even so, you should prod them to *rewrite* the expression. Their recall can be satisfying but it may undermine development of more advanced ideas that they can apply to computations that aren't easily recalled. An obvious way to make 6 + 9 is 5 + 10 or 10 + 5 in which one is given to 9 to make a 10. But, there are other ways. It might be thought of as 5 + 1 + 9, which is a similar idea. It might also be thought of as 6 + 6 + 3. In time, students might make it as 9 + 9 − 3. Though using subtraction hasn't been a highlighted strategy for decomposing numbers it can be useful. You should accept and lift it up when it happens.

> E
>
> How can you make
> ## 6 + 9?

F. The true power of flexibility in thinking about numbers becomes evident as addends become more complex. The same holds true for the other operations. Example F shows how you can modify this routine to go beyond basic facts. Here, students consider other ways to make 36 + 19, which may include 35 + 20 or 36 + 4 + 15. Students themselves might come up with even more resourceful ways to think about the expression. You should note that 36 + 19 clearly relates to the basic fact in Example E. For classes ready to work with 36 + 19 and similar expressions, you might first open with the related fact (6 + 9) so that students are poised to make connections to 36 + 19 that they might not do so on their own.

> F
>
> How can you make
> ## 36 + 19?

HOW CAN YOU MAKE IT? VARIATION—FRACTIONS AND DECIMALS

Proficiency with decomposing multi-digit numbers isn't necessarily the end goal. Students should have experiences decomposing and manipulating expressions as noted in the first variation (Examples E and F). Students can also learn to decompose other types of numbers including fractions and decimals.

G. Some students have experience decomposing fractions. They likely work to decompose fractions into a collection of unit fractions or other arrangements. They might decompose $\frac{5}{8}$ into $\frac{1}{8}+\frac{4}{8}$ or $\frac{3}{8}+\frac{2}{8}$. As with other fraction work, student experiences with fractions greater than one may be unbalanced or inadequate. Example G shows how you can modify the routine to have students decompose a mixed number. Here, they might break $1\frac{7}{8}$ into 1 and $\frac{7}{8}$, $\frac{6}{8}$ and $1\frac{1}{8}$, and so on. You might first have students work with fractions less than 1 before providing opportunities for them to decompose mixed numbers. Keep in mind that you should have them decompose mixed numbers beyond the whole and the fraction part.

> **G**
>
> How can you make
>
> $$1\frac{7}{8}?$$

H. Decomposing decimals has the same advantages as decomposing whole numbers. Example H presents a decimal number to be decomposed. Students might revert to *simple* strategies when working with decimals. That is, they might decompose by place value (10 + 4 + 0.5) or they might make *clean breaks* (14 + 0.5 or 10 + 4.5). As they show these preferences, you can once again restrict how numbers can be decomposed as mentioned in Example C. You can also help your students connect whole number decompositions with decimal decompositions by sequencing the routine intentionally. For example, fifth graders might be asked to decompose 145 in a variety of ways before shifting to 14.5. You might leave the decomposition of 145 on the board or screen for students to reference as they decompose 14.5.

> **H**
>
> How can you make
>
> 14.5?

THE MIGHTY TEN (COMBINATIONS OF TENS, HUNDREDS, OR THOUSANDS)

About the Routine

Incredibly important mathematical ideas are introduced and developed in primary grades. One of the most important ideas is the combinations of 10. Combinations of 10 serve as the groundwork for developing strategies for recalling basic facts. Combinations of 10 can be extended to making new tens like 24 and 6 makes 30 or 53 and 7 makes 60. Later in elementary mathematics, students build on their understanding of combinations that make 10 to make hundreds (350 and 50 makes 400) or thousands (600 and 400 makes 1,000). And later, students apply combinations of 10 to make 1 with tenths (0.3 and 0.7) or to make a tenth with hundredths (0.08 and 0.02). The most obvious application of this skill is to develop efficient computational strategies with multi-digit numbers. Combinations of 10 are clearly taught in primary grades. They are revisited from time to time, usually just before they are to be applied to a new topic. Yet, we cannot practice and extend such a critical skill enough. In fact, it's entirely possible that students in second, third, and fourth grades need to routinely practice combinations of 10 as well as connect combinations to making tens, to

Make 10		
6	4	1
7	5	2
3	8	4

making hundreds, to making thousands, and so on. In this routine, *The Mighty Ten*, students look for different combinations of 10. They discuss the combinations and then look for them again. Later in first grade through fourth grade, students first make combinations of 10 and then use those combinations to make other tens (see Example C and D). During that debrief, discussion highlights the relationships within the combinations (e.g., 6 + 4 is similar to 86 + 4).

online resources — All tasks can be downloaded for your use at **resources.corwin.com/ jumpstartroutines/elementary**

Why It Matters

This routine helps students:

- consider multiple combinations that make 10 (MP2);
- identify when a combination will not make 10 (MP2);
- develop strategies to improve precision when computing (MP6);
- gain comfort and confidence with number patterns and strategies so that tools are used strategically (MP5);
- determine patterns within number combinations for developing efficient computation strategies or shortcuts (MP8); and
- extend combinations of 10 to different numbers and/or place values (MP2).

What They Should Understand First

Students must understand that numbers can be decomposed into two (or more) numbers before working with *The Mighty Ten*. They must also understand that there can be more than one way to decompose any number. This is usually developed with smaller numbers, such as 5, first. Though not mentioned later as a variation, you could first present this routine as *The Mighty Five*. Students should be able to represent these combinations with tools before connecting those tools to symbolic (number) representations. Students may need to revisit tools, including number charts or base 10 models, as new combinations are introduced. Students at all levels should show some recognition of and comfort with patterns so that the patterns within combinations can be observed or discussed. Students do not need to fluently find these combinations. Instead, they should have strategies for finding combinations, including counting on by ones or counting back from ones. This routine intends to develop fluency with identifying combinations.

What to Do

1. Present a three-by-three grid with different digits appearing in each cell. Digits can be omitted or repeated. For example, the grid might have three 8s and no 4s. Also note that the grid can be changed to a four-by-four if necessary.

2. Have students find as many combinations of 10 as possible. (Note: Students can find combinations of more than two numbers (e.g., 5, 3, and 2 make 10).)

3. Have students share their combinations.

4. Record student combinations as expressions (e.g., 5 + 5). If possible, record combinations vertically with related combinations (5 + 5 and 6 + 4) adjacent to one another so that patterns can be observed.

5. Discuss combinations that students have shared.

6. Discuss class representations during or after recording ideas. Questions to ask might include:

   » How are the combinations related?
   » What patterns do you notice in the combinations?
   » Are there any combinations missing?
   » (Identify a combination) How could this combination (e.g., 5 + 5) help you think about 5 + 6?
   » (Identify a combination) What is a different problem that (this) combination could help you solve?
   » (Identify a combination of more than two numbers) How is this combination (e.g., 7 + 2 + 1) similar to 7 + 3?
   » Can you find another combination of 10 that has more than two numbers?
   » How can combinations of 10 help you when you add numbers?
   » How can combinations of 10 help when you subtract numbers?

7. Consider offering a new set of nine digits (in different locations) and asking students to find combinations of 10 again if time permits.

Anticipated Strategies for This Example

Make 10		
6	4	1
7	5	2
3	8	4

Students are likely to use tools, including their fingers, to find combinations. They may count on from a number or count back from 10. Others might show all 10 fingers to represent two groups and count the number in each group to identify a combination. With practice and experience, combinations should become more automatic. Even so, some combinations such as 7 and 3 may remain a challenge for students. There will be students who simply *know* the combinations. These students can benefit from the routine by searching for combinations made with more than two numbers. In some classes, students will be ready for making other tens almost immediately. You can accelerate those students to versions similar to Example C or D. As you pose new combinations (combinations of 20, 30, or 40) to students, it's possible that they will revert to one-to-one counting to find those combinations. Keep in mind that students might need these strategies. You can shape discussions so that connections to the basic combinations of 10 are made.

THE MIGHTY TEN—ADDITIONAL EXAMPLES

A. Students need many opportunities to practice combinations of 10 in order to develop automatic recall of them. For young mathematicians, they must first make sense of how numbers are combined. Picking digits out of a table is unlikely to be an appropriate place to begin with them. Instead, these students can use representations of numbers to build capacity with this concept. Example A shows how this can happen. Here, students are presented with three 10 frame cards and asked to find a combination of 10. In time, you can display a fourth and possibly a fifth 10 frame card. Note that the representation of 6 doesn't fill a row with one more and that the representation of 4 is also slightly different. This is intentional so that students are exposed to various ways that numbers can be represented. You want them to understand that 6 is still 6 regardless of what it looks like. You can use these variants of representation at your discretion. Also note that 10 frame cards are provided as a downloadable resource.

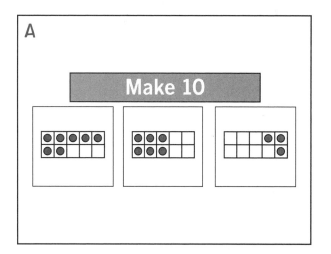

online resources ☝ Ten Frame Cards can be downloaded for your use at resources.corwin.com/jumpstartroutines/elementary

You can copy them, cut them out, and present them to students with a document camera instead of through PowerPoint slides.

B. We have to rearrange how numbers are displayed on 10 frames so that students make sense of number rather than simply memorize an arrangement. Young students should also experience numbers represented in other ways than 10 frames. Example B shows what this might look like. Here, students are presented with four dot cards and are asked to make 10 again. You can download dot cards and use them as explained with 10 frame cards above. You can also choose to use dominos or domino cards as well. You should look for students who count by ones to make combinations of 10 and those who count on from a number and even those students who begin to *see the combinations*. You should be sure to record addition equations that connect to the combinations of 10 regardless of student exposure to or experience with equations. You might also consider providing Unifix® or linking cubes to students so that they can build models of the tens.

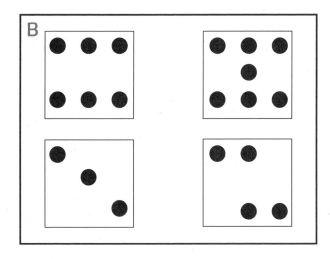

C. The power of *The Mighty Ten* becomes evident as versions like Example C are offered to classes. Here, students must extend their understanding of combinations of 10 to make combinations of 40. They transfer the combination of 3 and 7 to 33 and 7. It seems like an obvious connection. However, many students do not always make those connections between combinations of 10 and related expressions. Students who can recall combinations of 10 effortlessly and even recall most, if not all, of the basic facts can face this challenge of transfer. Upon reflection, it makes sense because these combinations are not often a focal point of practice. The example can be simply changed to make any other number like 50 or 70. In time, you can modify the example so that combinations are extended to teen numbers. For example, you could ask students to make 60 with 43 and 17 or 48 and 12 by using 40, 10, and 8 and 2, which make another 10.

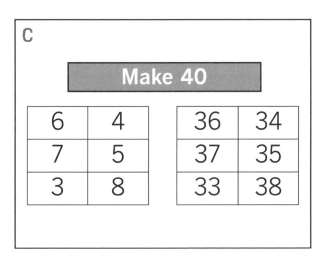

D. Using teen numbers in combinations, as mentioned just above, is one way you can adapt and extend combinations of tens to new situations. You can just as easily apply the change to three and four-digit number combinations. Example D shows how you might modify *The Mighty Ten* to expose your students to these ideas. Here, students are asked to make 750 when a set of numbers are single-digit numbers and the other set of numbers are in the 740s. Again, seemingly fluent students might be challenged to make and take advantage of the relationships. The routine has limitless possibilities. You might cleverly first use basic combinations of 10 example, followed by combinations of 80, followed by combinations of 380 so that patterns and relationships become blatantly obvious for your students. During discussion, you can then reinforce these patterns or point them out to students if they go unnoticed.

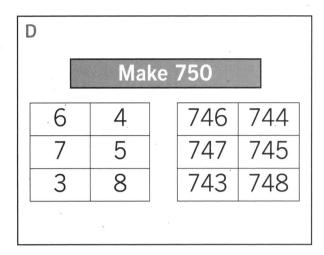

NOTES

THE MIGHTY TEN VARIATION—DECIMALS

For many students, computation with decimals becomes a procedural endeavor. This might be attributed to preference or it might be their perspective. It might be related to comfort with algorithms. Unfortunately, it might also be associated with a less than complete understanding of decimals as numbers with relationships similar to whole numbers. Students can *play* with decimals in ways that they play with whole numbers. You can retool *The Mighty Ten* to provide such an experience.

E. Example E is practically identical to the original example that would be used with students in first grade and possibly earlier. The only difference is that a decimal point has been added to each cell and the prompt has changed from make 10 to make one. But as noted above, many students will be challenged to find these combinations at first. To make matters worse, they may not be able to rely on their fingers to support them as they are no longer thinking about or using whole numbers. In essence, they haven't made connections or haven't had opportunities to make connections. You should resist the urge to only use money connotations to support students if possible. Instead, you can help them see connections to combinations of 10 through your questions and discussion.

E

Make 1		
.6	.4	.1
.7	.5	.2
.3	.8	.4

F. Example F extends combinations of 10 from tenths to hundredths. Again, you can be clever by first having students make combinations of 10 with whole numbers, followed by combinations of 1, and then combinations of hundredths. In other cases, it might make sense to make combinations of 10, 100, and 1,000 before shifting to tenths and hundredths. Doing so might uncover difficulties your students have transferring the notion of combinations of 10 to other place values not simply decimal place values. Practice with *The Mighty Ten* using decimal numbers will help develop fluency with these combinations, which in turn helps students develop efficient computational strategies for decimals.

F

Make a Tenth		
.06	.04	.01
.07	.05	.02
.03	.08	.04

THE MIGHTY TEN VARIATION—10 AND SOME MORE

The combinations of 10 are anchors for making sense of other combinations. If we know that 6 and 4 make 10, then 6 and 5 must be 1 more or 11. Making 10 and some more is another practical application of knowing combinations of 10. So, knowing that 9 and 1 make 10, 9 and 8 must make 17 because 1 can be given from 8 to 9 resulting in 10 and 7.

G. Example G shows how *The Mighty Ten* can be manipulated to extend understanding of making 10. Here, students are asked to find combinations of numbers that make more than 10. Debriefing discussions should focus on how a related expression is a known 10. For example, 6 and 5 are more than 10 because we know that 6 and 4 are 10. Discussions could also focus on how students use a known 10 to find the greater number. For example, 8 and 5 are more than 10 because 8 and 2 *are* 10. Students might think about 8 and 5 as 8 and 2 (10) and 3 more is 13. You can also modify this version of the routine like Example C where students are prompted with a group of single-digit numbers and a group of two-digit numbers. Then, you could prompt them to identify combinations that would yield numbers greater than the next 10. Example C would change from *make 40* to *make more than 40*.

G

Make More Than 10		
6	4	1
7	5	2
3	8	4

H. Example H builds on the 10 and some more modification in Example G. Instead, it asks students to identify combinations that will be more than 100. Thinking about combinations in these ways, as well as predicting results, helps students develop strategies for determining if their solutions are reasonable. Looking closely, you can see that Example H offers numbers in the 40s and 50s. This is intentional. 40 and 50 are 90. To be greater than 100, students will have to consider how 40, 50, and a new 10 or more than a new 10 are made. You could tweak this example to build on this concept by using numbers in the 30s and 60s, 20s and 70s, or 10s and 80s.

H

Make More Than 100		
46	54	41
47	55	58
53	48	44

MAKE IT FRIENDLY (COMPATIBLE NUMBERS)

About the Routine

As students develop proficiency with combinations of 10 through *The Mighty Ten* (Routine 8, page 69), we can soon have them apply their understanding to find sums of other numbers. They can even apply this skill to finding the sum of three or more numbers. Often when adding three numbers, students add more than two numbers in sequence without looking for compatible or friendly numbers. Yet, as we know, numbers can be rearranged to create compatible numbers. Doing this is a sign of refined number sense and emerging computational fluency. Typically, making 10 is the chief compatible to make but other combinations, including doubles, can be equally helpful. In this routine, *Make It Friendly*, students are presented with collections of numbers and asked to find the total. Throughout the routine, three numbers are provided for students to combine. It's possible that you could pose four and possibly five numbers. But, you might reserve this number of addends for students with well-developed computational strategies and sense of number. When you use three numbers, some students will combine from left to right and some others might combine from right to left. It's possible that

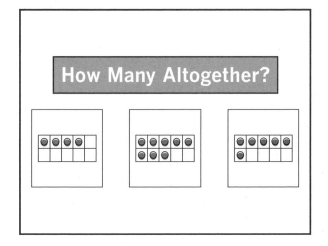

some students will look for the greatest number and add the next greatest number before adding the third. Of course, some students will look for compatibles or friendlies. You should prompt for an estimated sum before students find their sum. Estimating sums helps students develop their number sense, which supports their ability to determine if solutions are reasonable. You can even choose to discuss estimation strategies. You can also weave in new estimation strategies such as finding *too high* and *too low* estimates or other strategies that are unfamiliar to students.

Why It Matters

This routine helps students:

- develop efficient, flexible computation strategies (MP2);
- determine reasonableness of solutions by estimating results (MP2);
- consider number strategies of others (MP3);
- create arguments to justify their strategies (MP3);
- bolster number and computation strategies so that tools, including paper and pencil, are used strategically (MP5);
- increase the precision of their calculations (MP6);
- use patterns and structure to develop efficient strategies (MP7); and
- build confidence in their ability to do mathematics.

What They Should Understand First

The featured example of *Make It Friendly* would be perfect for first grade students. Students first working with these ideas should engage with representations that help build competence with rearranging or shifting numbers. A 10 frame is used in this example. Before working with the routine, students should be able to represent and manipulate diverse representations of numbers. Clearly, these students should have mastered concepts of counting and addition. Students should be familiar with combinations of 10 but do not need to be fluent with the combinations. The routine itself, in conjunction with others like *The Mighty Ten*, can build that fluency. Ideally, students working with this early version of the routine would be able to combine some numbers without needing to count on by ones. This too is not required and will be enhanced as they have more and more intentional number experiences.

What to Do

1. Present three numbers represented with 10 frames, dot cards, base 10 blocks, or symbolically.

2. Have students estimate the combined total and share their estimates with partners and the class.

3. Solicit and discuss estimates. During the discussion, questions to ask might include:
   - How did you make your estimate?
   - How are our estimates related?
   - What would be an estimate that is too low?
   - What would be an estimate that would be too high?
   - What would be a really bad estimate? Why?

4. After discussing estimates, have students find the exact sum.

5. Have students share their solutions and strategies with partners.

6. Discuss group strategies for finding the sum. Questions to ask might include:
   - How did you find the total?
   - Were there any numbers that could be combined easily?
   - How did those combinations help you add the numbers?
   - How else could we order the numbers to add them?
   - Would a different order of adding the numbers be more or less efficient?
   - How does our exact sum compare to our estimates?

7. Acknowledge and praise student reasoning and perseverance.

Anticipated Strategies for This Example

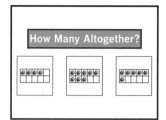

The routine intends for students to see numbers and make decisions about combining them efficiently. Students might be challenged to do this initially. In the featured 10 frame example, students might begin with 4 and count on eight more (12) and then count on six more (18). This strategy signifies two important thoughts. The first is that they believe that they must add the numbers in order of appearance. It also signals that these students rely on counting by ones. Some students might begin with the largest number on the middle 10 frame before counting on by ones. These students might move to 6 next. Others might begin with 8 before adding from left to right. The most efficient strategy is to make a 10 from the first and last 10 frames and then add on seven more. It's likely that at least one student will recognize this efficiency. It's also possible that no students will use this strategy in initial forays into the routine. In these cases, you need to inject this idea and ask students to think if it will always work. Moreover, you should revisit this strategy as needed before using the routine again on subsequent days.

MAKE IT FRIENDLY—ADDITIONAL EXAMPLES

A. As noted in other routines, students must be able to recognize and represent numbers in a variety of ways. The featured example shows how this routine can play out with 10 frame cards. Example A shows how you can adjust it to make use of dot cards. There is another, more significant difference with this example. Here, they are to find the total of 6, 5, and 6. None of the three numbers are combinations of 10. Instead, students will have to rely on an adjusting or compensation strategy. They might give four from the middle card to the first card making a 10 before adding on one and then six more. Other students might also give four but simultaneously give one to the other six creating 10 and 7. Students may even use basic fact strategies as they learn about them. For this example, students might double six for 12 before adding five more. In doing so, students might double quite easily but still need to add on five by counting ones. It is also important to note that as strategies and skills evolve, 10 frame and dot card representations should be eventually replaced with symbolic numbers only.

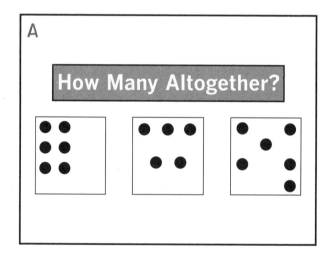

B. Second and third grade students, even fourth and fifth graders can develop advanced strategies by using this routine. Some may need to work with single digits first but soon they can work with two- and three-digit addends. But, like younger students, they can first work with pictorial representations of these numbers. Example B shows how they might be introduced to two-digit numbers represented with sticks and dots. Again, you should ask students to estimate before having them work to find the sum. It would also be wise for you to first record the numbers just below the dot cards. To find how many, students might count by tens before counting by ones. Some might count by groups of tens before counting by ones. In any case, students will have to make decisions about how they will combine ones. Also note that the middle card is an intentional representation. Some students may not recognize it as 39. This gives you an idea about other concepts you might have to revisit.

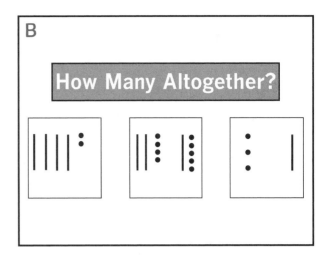

C. Example B mentions that stick and dot cards should accompany the symbolic representations of the numbers. In time, you should remove the pictorial representations leaving only the symbolic. Example C shows what that would look like. Initial work with two-digit numbers might cause students to return to low-level, sequential adding strategies. These students might even use partial sums to do so. When this happens, it is vital that you also highlight other ways for numbers to be combined. In this example, 49 and 41 might be added first by thinking of them as 40, 40, and 10 or 90. Adding 28 to 90 gives students an opportunity to apply a different decomposition strategy to make a new 10 (100) with 18 left over.

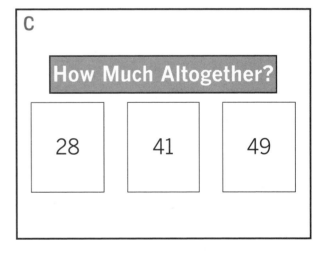

D. Obviously, making tens have been featured so far in this routine. It is a highly useful strategy. Decomposing and adding partials is also quite useful. Yet, in some cases it's better to make compatible numbers. 25 and 75 are examples of compatible numbers. They are instantly recognizable as 100. Example D shows how you can adjust *Make It Friendly* to help students look for and use other compatible numbers. In this example, they are prompted with 19, 74, and 25. Students could distribute six to 74 and five to 25 but that can be problematic as it requires them to mentally retain a lot of information. Essentially, there are too many moving parts. But, students could use other compatibles. They could give one from 19 to 74 to make 75. Then, the problem becomes 18, 75, and 25, which makes it easier to find 118. You might reserve work with these relatively more advanced compatibles and friendlies for later experiences.

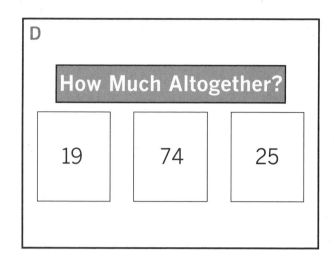

NOTES

MAKE IT FRIENDLY VARIATION—FINDING DIFFERENCES

There are times when students need to subtract two numbers from another number. However, there aren't many instances in which students build fluency with strategies for subtracting more than one number from another. You can modify *Make It Friendly* to do this. In this modification, students are asked "How many are left?" so that the two right numbers are subtracted from the first number. This modification might not be best suited for students before third grade though each and every student is different.

E. Example E shows what "How Much?" might look like with subtraction. Here, students are prompted to find how much is left when 53 and 38 are taken away from 98. As with addition, students might first subtract 53 followed by 38 overlooking the relationship between 98 and 38. Students might be more apt to *find* the convenience of subtracting 38 first if 53 created a regrouping situation. Nonetheless, students can subtract in order from left to right. But, the routine intends for students to think about efficiency and compatibility. Taking 38 from 98 results in 60 creating a difference of 60 and 53, which is 7. Also note that students might use partial differences to subtract *straight across* the numbers. You should acknowledge and praise the approach and compare it with using compatibles so that students widen their repertoire of computation strategies.

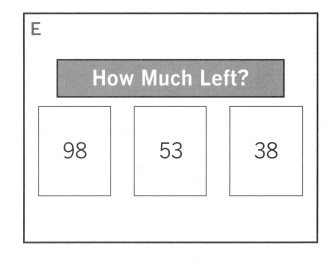

F. Example F is similar to Example E. In it, students are again asked to find how much is left when 17 and 23 are subtracted from 61. The numbers presented in this version of the routine might elicit a different strategy altogether. Some students figure that when subtracting two numbers from a third requires one subtraction followed by another. However, one can also add the two numbers to be subtracted before taking the sum from the minuend. Here, students might find it more efficient to combine 17 and 23 (50) before subtracting from 61. Clearly, 61 − 50 is much easier to think about than 61 − 17 − 23. This strategy may not be obvious at first because the numbers themselves don't present an obvious need to combine. You can manipulate numbers in the routine so that apparent efficiencies *emerge*. For example, 17 and 23 might not be obvious compatibles but 25 and 25 are. Imagine how your students might respond if presented with 61, 25, and 25 in this routine. It is highly likely that at least one student will *discover* this strategy of adding numbers before subtracting them.

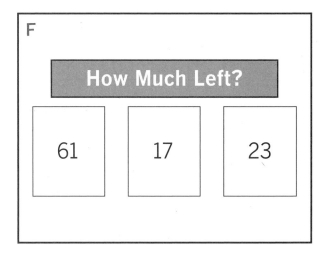

MAKE IT FRIENDLY VARIATION—FRACTIONS

Many students will benefit greatly from work with this routine simply using whole numbers. But, you can easily adjust it to develop fluency with adding fractions for your fourth or fifth graders. Examples G and H show what that might look like.

G. Example G offers three fractions with like denominators. Making 10 is a convenient, friendly number for adding whole numbers. Making 1 or any other whole number is convenient when adding fractions. Again, students should first estimate the sum of the fractions before finding exacts. They might estimate using only the relationship to more or less than $\frac{1}{2}$, one whole, or two wholes rather than estimating an exact amount such as $1\frac{3}{8}$. In this example, students might combine $3\frac{2}{4}$ to then need to add $\frac{5}{4}$ twice. But, another approach might be to decompose $\frac{5}{4}$ giving $\frac{3}{4}$ to the amount on the left and $\frac{2}{4}$ to the amount on the right leaving two quantities equal to 1.

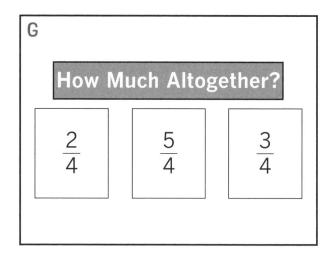

H. Example H does not have like denominators. There are still ways that students can think about friendly adjustments in order to find the sum more easily. Students could give $\frac{1}{8}$ from $\frac{5}{8}$ to create 1, $\frac{4}{8}$, and $\frac{1}{2}$. Other students might quickly recognize that $\frac{1}{2}$ is equivalent to $\frac{4}{8}$ and then decompose and redistribute in a variety of ways. You can adjust and modify *Make It Friendly* in all sorts of ways to help students develop fraction fluency. You can add a fourth fraction. You can use mixed numbers. You can present like or unlike denominators, or you can change it so that students find differences with fractions.

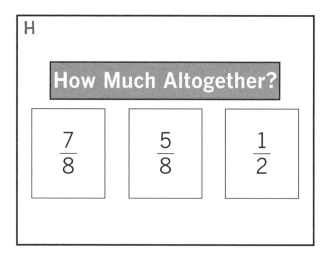

MYSTERY NUMBER (NUMBER CONCEPTS AND RELATIONSHIPS)

About the Routine

Every number has attributes that make it unique. A number can be even or odd. It can have number of tens and ones or hundreds, tens, and ones. It can be represented in a variety of ways with a variety of tools. It is a sum and a difference at the same time. It is half of another number and twice as much of a different number. The possibilities are endless. Yet, students sometimes perceive numbers to have relatively few attributes. Or, students might see each of these number concepts as unique, disconnected ideas. Learning and understanding mathematics as an isolated collection of concepts is described as instrumental learning or understanding (Skemp, 2006). But, mathematics can be understood, and understood well, through relational understanding. It describes learning as building understanding through making connections and seeing relationships between concepts or skills. When students learn about mathematics by making connections, they are much more likely to be successful. However, students also need opportunities to practice and reinforce their familiarity with these relationships. Jump-start routines are intended to develop specific skills with numbers, including counting, magnitude,

comparison, estimation, and computation. Routines can also be used to develop a robust network of relational understanding. *Mystery Number* is a routine to *play* with commonalities and differences of numbers through a collection of clues. However, it is not quite a traditional riddle-type activity. Instead, students engage with one clue after another making refinements to their guesses based on each new revelation. It helps students see the many dimensions of a number and the many possibilities for a given attribute of numbers.

> ### The Mystery Number
> - is less than 50
> - is greater than 18
> - is made with a 3
> - is not made with a 4
> - is between 20 and 30

 All tasks can be downloaded for your use at **resources.corwin.com/jumpstartroutines/elementary**

Why It Matters

This routine helps students:

- make sense of problems and open-ended prompts (MP1);
- persevere through mathematics problems as conditions change and new solutions need to be considered (MP1);
- develop understanding of attributes of numbers (MP2);
- see patterns within and relationships among numbers (MP7);
- justify their solutions (MP3); and
- accept the arguments of others if/when their solutions are different (MP3).

What They Should Understand First

Mystery Number intends to help students better understand various concepts about numbers. Students should be introduced to concepts formally before experiencing them in the routine. In the featured example, students should be able to compare numbers to other numbers in order to determine that the mystery number is less than 50 and greater than 18. Students should understand place value so that they can make sense of the middle clues. Students must accept that there can be more than one possibility for a given prompt. You can develop this by frequently using open-ended questions during your instruction. You can also develop this by avoiding unintentional messages that there are preferred or singular ways for solving a problem. Note that the routine aims to support students' thinking and flexibility of thought. Some students may be able to think flexibly in certain instances (there are many numbers less than 50) while not being able to think as flexibly about how many numbers have a 3 in them (numbers can have three tens or three ones).

What to Do

1. Write a collection of clues that represent a number. Keep in mind that it may be easier to identify a number first and then write clues about that number.

2. Present one clue about the mystery number at a time. (Note: The downloadable slides are designed so that clues transition in one after another on a mouse click or pointer advance. This may need adjusting due to differences in computers and software applications.)

3. Have students identify a possibility for the clue and share their thinking with a partner.

4. Solicit and record student solutions for the first clue.

5. Discuss how each of the solutions relate to the clue.

6. Present the next clue. Direct students to identify a new solution or explain why their first solution still satisfies the second clue.

7. With the class, eliminate original numbers that no longer satisfy the two clues.

8. Solicit and record new solutions.

9. Repeat this process with subsequent clues.

10. Be sure to highlight how numbers satisfy the clues. Questions to ask during the discussions include:

   » How does (number) satisfy each of the clues?

   » How is this number similar to the other numbers that satisfying the clues?

   » What next clue might eliminate (one of these numbers)?

11. Celebrate student perseverance and solution finding.

Anticipated Strategies for This Example

The Mystery Number is

• less than 50
• greater than 18
• made with a 3
• not made with a 4
• between 20 and 30

The list of student strategies for engaging with the featured example are endless. Students are first prompted to think about a number less than 50. They might count back by ones or tens to identify their offering. Some will instantly think of a number. You should be cognizant of students who choose one or two less than 50 as they may have underdeveloped thoughts about comparison and relationship. Keep in mind that identifying 48 or 49 does not automatically indicate this limitation. In other cases, students might identify numbers in the forties without considering numbers from other decades. These students might have slightly better developed ideas but may still be challenged to think beyond 10 less than a number. The second clue, greater than 18, may not eliminate many solutions but the third likely will. Again, you should be on the lookout for students who appear to have narrow thoughts about numbers with a 3 in them. Some might think that a number must be in the thirties. While others might think it will only have a 3 in the ones place. Some students might be challenged to string clues together in that they land on 13 as a number with a 3 in it, but don't reconcile that it also must be more than 18.

MYSTERY NUMBER—ADDITIONAL EXAMPLES

A. You can play *Mystery Number* in any grade. The numbers and clues will change but the benefits will be similar. Example A shows what *Mystery Number* might look like in kindergarten. It's quite likely that many kindergarten students will be unable to read the clues. You can still present them, though you might need to use drawings and representations to support the written clue. As you read the clues, you can also discuss important ideas being within the clues. Here, students first have to think about numbers that are made with one 10 frame. You might provide students with magnetic 10 frames or lapboards to use during the routine. As with the featured example, students make a number and discuss how it satisfies the first clue. The second clue introduces a new idea describing the mystery number as greater than 5. Now, some students will have to adjust their thinking. Subsequent clues narrow the possibilities while helping students think about numbers in different ways. You can adjust clues for this grade level to include one more, two more, one less, and two less. You might also provide pictorial clues, for example use a picture of counters in place of the written clues.

A

The Mystery Number

• is made with one ten frame
• is more than 5
• is not one more than 6
• is not one less than 8
• is one less than 10

B. Example B shows how you can use *Mystery Number* in first grade. It can be inefficient for students to model clues with physical tools. Tools might also undermine the mental framework of relational understanding we want students to develop. You have to judge when a tool helps or hinders students' thinking. Some tools like number charts might be helpful for students to keep track of their progress through the clues while building relational understanding. For instance, each student might have a copy of a 100 chart to cross off numbers as new clues are provided. Seeing the digits of the numbers can also help students make sense of and process each new clue. Example B also shows how clues can begin to become more complex. The third clue states that the sum of the digits of the mystery number is 11. Now, students are no longer simply thinking about numbers by their place value or through simple comparison. This shows how you might weave in ideas about computation. You should note that these types of clues might be reserved for the second or third quarters of first grade dependent upon the mathematical maturity of your students.

C. Clues for *Mystery Number* are limited only by your resourcefulness and creativity. There are no limits. Example C introduces notions of skip-counting into the routine. This might be a good clue for some time in second or third grade. The clues you use should be related to skills or concepts that students have already learned about. But, students don't have to master those skills or concepts. You might use this skip-counting clue shortly after introducing the concept. Doing this may help your students integrate new skills and concepts with less effort, more quickly, or with more *sticking power*.

B

The Mystery Number

- is between 50 and 80
- is not 10 more than 63
- has 11 as the sum of its digits
- has 7 tens

C

The Mystery Number

- is said when skip-counting
- has a 5 in it
- is less than 80
- has digits that are a sum of 10
- is halfway between 50 and 60

D. As Example C notes, there is really no limit to the type, quality, or concept of a clue. Here, a basic fact is introduced as a clue. Example D offers another unique twist on the routine. The clues do not result in one exact answer. The result could be any number in the twenties or 32. This is useful for you to keep in mind for two reasons. First, it helps students become comfortable with multiple *final* solutions. This can be disruptive for students who perceive math to always have one right answer. It also provides flexibility for you to end a routine that might be running too long. It is important to remember that you control the first few minutes of mathematics class rather than your students. Some clues will create a wonderful discussion that might linger. Other clues might be tough for students to make sense of and might linger. When this happens, you can omit the last clue or two so that the routine can end in a timely manner.

D

The Mystery Number

- is even
- is more than 9 + 9
- has a 2 in it
- is less than 40

NOTES

_____

_____

_____

_____

_____

_____

_____

_____

_____

_____

_____

_____

_____

_____

MYSTERY NUMBER VARIATION—MULTI-DIGIT NUMBERS

You can modify *Mystery Number* to meet any of your students' needs. Naturally, you can tune it to help your students think relationally about three- and four-digit numbers. Five- and six-digit numbers as well as decimal numbers and fractions are also options. Like a handful of other routines, you can use *Mystery Number* with geometry or measurement and data concepts in elementary mathematics.

E. Example E shows how *Mystery Number* might work with three-digit numbers. It also highlights a different clue that hasn't been shared in earlier examples. Here, ideas of rounding are posed in the third and fourth clues. You can also use clues to complement other ideas about estimation. Instead of a rounding clue, you might use a clue like "the mystery number is close to the benchmark 200." Clues about rounding and benchmarks help students think about number relationships and strengthen their thoughts about estimating.

E

The Mystery Number

- is more than 300
- has one 7 and one 6 in it
- rounds to 400
- rounds to 380

F. Example F has a mystery number that is four digits. The first clue frames comparison differently by sharing that the mystery number is less than half of 8,000. This is simply another way to say less than 4,000, but it causes students to think about it in a distinctly different way. Again, there are no limits to the clues you might use in *Mystery Number*. As your students gain familiarity with the routine, you can even position them as the author the clues. To do this, you might give students numbers on index cards and have them write clues about the numbers on the back. You can collect those cards and use them in later versions of the routine. You might even share student generated works with colleagues to use with their students.

F

The Mystery Number

- is less than half of 8,000
- is more than 2,000
- has two 3s
- has two 4s
- is odd

MYSTERY NUMBER VARIATION—BASIC FACTS

There is little doubt that thinking about how numbers are related is helpful for both a deeper and broader mathematical understanding. Relational thinking should be applied to other skills and concepts as well. This may be most useful when developing computational fluency and basic fact recall. Success with each of these stems from understanding how numbers are related and how they can be manipulated.

G. Examples G and H offer *Mystery Facts*. Instead of giving clues for a specific number, these examples give clues for a basic fact. Otherwise, the routine plays out in exactly the same way. For the first clue in Example G, students might conjure 4 + 2, 5 + 2, or 9 + 2. After the second clue, 4 + 2 and 5 + 2 would be eliminated but 8 + 2 could be added to the list if not already considered. The third clue eliminates 9 + 2 while the fourth confirms that it is 8 + 2. It would also be interesting to see if students recognize that the mystery fact could be either 8 + 2 or 2 + 8. Some will come to this conclusion easily. Others might interpret two-more facts quite narrowly thinking that only the second addend can be 2.

G
The Mystery Fact   • is a two-more fact   • is a two-digit sum   • is made with two even addends   • is a make-ten fact

H. The basic facts used in this version of the routine should be part of fact sets that the students have been exposed to. It will work with addition or subtraction and multiplication or division. Example H shares clues about a multiplication fact. It also does well to reinforce other important ideas. The first clue states that the mystery fact has an odd product. This becomes an opportunity to talk about what must be true about the factors (both are odd). Students who offer facts that have one or two even factors may be signaling that they haven't mastered this concept. Though the second clue simply gives a range for the product, it in effect limits the possibilities for students to consider to 3 × 9 and 5 × 7. The third clue builds on the patterns within products and factors as well as the relationships between fact sets. As we know, ×5 facts are related to ×10 facts. This combined with the other three clues warrant the fourth clue unnecessary. Even so, it can be revealed to ratify the conclusion of 5 × 7.

H
The Mystery Fact   • has an odd product   • is product between 25 and 40   • is related to a ×10 fact   • has a product in the 30s

NUMBER BIO (NUMBER CONCEPTS AND RELATIONSHIPS)

About the Routine

Every number has a story to tell. Numbers fall into shared categories in that they are even or odd or greater or less than 50. Each number is also unique. *Number Bio* (biography) is a routine for students to reinforce their understanding about numbers. It helps them think about how to decompose numbers. It helps them think about how a number relates to other numbers or how that number might be represented with a 10 frame or on a number line. *Number Bio* is a different type of routine in that it doesn't deal explicitly with number sense and reasoning. Instead, it helps students think about different aspects of number and number relationships so that they are more comfortable and confident. In this routine, you present students with a number and a set of conditions to complete relative to that number. There is no limit to the size or type of number nor the number of conditions that students must address. You can print and copy *Number Bio* recording sheets and place them in plastic page protectors so that they can be reused each day for a week or so.

 Templates for the routine are available through the downloadable content for this book. Or, you can easily create your own. In fact, the routine could be completed without

copying recording sheets at all. Students could fold a regular piece of copy paper in half repeatedly to make sections for recording their thinking. Students could also draw lines on their personal whiteboards to create sections. After completing the prompts in each section, students share solutions with a partner. Some conditions, such as even or odd, have only one answer. But other conditions, such as showing the number on a number line, have a range of possibilities.

A Number Bio for 28

Ten more	Break it apart	A number that is more and a number that is less
Ten less	Show it with sticks and dots	On a number line

All tasks can be downloaded for your use at **resources.corwin.com/ jumpstartroutines/elementary**

Why It Matters

This routine helps students:

- make sense of closed and open-ended prompts about numbers (MP1);
- persevere through mathematics problems as conditions change and new solutions need to be considered (MP1);
- develop understanding of attributes of numbers (MP2);
- use representations to communicate their thinking (MP3);
- see patterns within and relationships among numbers (MP7);
- accept the arguments of others if/when their solutions are different (MP3); and
- reinforce understanding of diverse number concepts.

What They Should Understand First

The *Number Bio* in the featured example would be perfect for any time in first grade. Students should have some understanding of the various concepts presented in the organizer. Some of the prompts will have single, correct answers. Others will have multiple possibilities, which might be challenging for students. This is especially true for placements on number lines and base 10 models. Students should be able to represent numbers with diverse base 10 models, including 10 frames, base 10 blocks, or sticks and dots. You can replace number lines with number paths if needed. Either way, students should be able to find numbers on a number line and explain how number lines work. You can strengthen student understanding of number lines through routines, including *Where's the Point?* (Routine 13, page 102) and *Is This the End?* (Routine 14, page 109). You might provide number charts or 100 charts to students as they work to complete their *Number Bio* organizers. But, you might want to reserve those tools to confirm solutions during discussion.

What to Do

1. Identify a number and prompts or conditions about the number for students to complete. Consider creating an anchor chart for the routine to use with the class.

2. Have students complete each of the conditions for the number.

3. Have students share their solutions with a partner.

4. Bring the class together to share solutions.

5. Record student solutions with the anchor chart referenced above. Avoid students coming up one at a time to record their solutions as this can have a negative impact on timing and student engagement.

6. Discuss how students thought of or found solutions for the different conditions. During discussion, questions to ask (for this example) might include:

   » How did you think of 10 more and 10 less?

   » Are there other ways to find 10 more and 10 less?

   » How is 10 more and 10 less represented on the number chart?

   » What patterns do you notice in 10 more and 10 less of numbers?

   » How did you know how many sticks and dots to make?

   » What do the sticks and dots represent?

   » Could the sticks and dots be represented in another way?

   » Are there other ways to break apart or decompose 28?

- » How are the ways we decomposed 28 similar and different?
- » How are our number lines similar and different?
- » Could 28 go on a number line with different endpoints?

7. Consider limiting conditions to complete, explore, and/or discuss due to time limitations. Make note of conditions that are skipped or determine conditions that are priorities to explore.

8. Celebrate student success and effort.

Anticipated Strategies for This Example

A Number Bio for 28		
Ten more	Break it apart	A number that is more and a number that is less
Ten less	Show it with sticks and dots	On a number line

Even closed prompts, such as 10 more and 10 less, can tell you quite a bit about student thinking and understanding. Some students might complete this section by counting on and counting back by ones to find their solutions. Other students might recognize a pattern while others rely on a number chart. Students are likely to use two sticks and eight dots to show 28. Yet, some students might rearrange the sticks and dots showing a stick, three dots, another stick, and then five dots. These representations are important discussion opportunities as it can help all students think about the meaning of the representation instead of memorizing what a number *looks like*. Student representations on the number lines can be quite telling about their perspectives as well. Some number lines may be open with endpoints of 0 and 100. Other number lines might be ticked that count from 20 to 30. Of course, there are a host of other possibilities. This is just one example of how a condition in *Number Bio* can be used for a rich conversation about numbers, representations, and relationships.

NUMBER BIO—ADDITIONAL EXAMPLES

A. *Number Bio* has practical uses in kindergarten as well as first grade. Example A shows what the routine might look like with single-digit numbers and early number concepts. Students are asked to think about one more and one less than 9. These are closed, single-answer conditions. But like the featured example, you can offer prompts with many different possible responses. You can also leverage the routine so that students are forced to think about how an individual tool or model can be manipulated. For example, you can ask students to show 9 on the 10 frame. Then, you can ask them to show 9 on the 10 frame in a different way. Group discussion can focus on how each representation of nine is different and how each is the same. Representing other single-digit numbers on a 10 frame offer diverse possibilities too. Six can be shown with a top row of 5 and one more, a bottom row of 5 and one more, or two *stacks* of 3. This featured example also introduces dominos and the bottom right example puts the number into the context of the real-world as students might have nine crayons in their pencil boxes or nine buttons on their shirts.

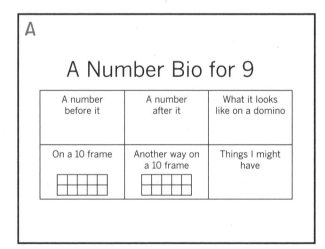

A

A Number Bio for 9

A number before it	A number after it	What it looks like on a domino
On a 10 frame	Another way on a 10 frame	Things I might have

B. Like the featured example, Example B would work well in first grade. It is provided to give new perspectives about the conditions of two-digit numbers that students might be asked. It is worth taking note of the prompt in this example that asks if the number is close to 0, 50, or 100. This prompt exposes students to ideas about how numbers are related to important benchmarks. The bottom left is another example of a relationship question that students can consider. Rounding is not something that first graders typically work with but they can think about how a number is close to 70 or 80. The bottom middle prompt shows how 10 more and 10 less might evolve into other more and less considerations. You might include certain big ideas, such as decomposition and number line representation, in every version of *Number Bio*.

B

A Number Bio for 77

Is close to 0, 50, or 100	Break it apart	Break apart a different way
The TEN that it is closest to	5 more and 5 less	On a number line

C. Three-digit numbers can be introduced and reinforced in second grade versions of *Number Bio*. In those versions, such as Example C, students can continue to reference charts and other tools to confirm the accuracy of their solutions. The upper right condition in Example C shows how addition can be woven into the routine. In that cell, students are asked what the sum of the featured number (265) and 125 is. The bottom right condition, how much more to 1,000, can be found with subtraction or by counting up. Student discussion about how these conditions were satisfied will help everyone think about how they can add and subtract with these larger numbers.

C

A Number Bio for 265

Is close to 0, 500, or 1,000	Break it apart	Added to 125
The closest hundred	10, 100, and 200 more	How much more to 1,000?

D. Example D offers four-digit numbers for the routine. It might be used in third grade or fourth grade. The conditions prompted about 4,028 draw attention to things colleagues might look for in earlier grades. For example, the bottom left and bottom center cells ask students directly to represent the number on two different number lines. This example poses a unique condition in that 4,028 is the sum of two numbers. Of course, conditions from featured first grade examples could be applied to this four-digit number. You can swap out the conditions however you like or charge your students with creating conditions to include in the prompt. The flexibility of the routine enables it to be a perfect tool for spiral review of critical concepts.

D

A Number Bio for 4,028

Rounded to the nearest ten, hundred, and thousand	Is about halfway between	Break it apart
On a number line	On a number line with different endpoints	Is the sum of these two numbers

NUMBER BIO VARIATION—BASIC FACTS AND COMPUTATION

Numbers have common characteristics. Basic facts do as well. Students can use ideas about basic facts and relationships between facts to help them recall facts and determine if their solutions are accurate. Students can explore multi-digit computations in similar ways.

E. Strategies for recalling basic facts are a focus of our instruction. The first cell in Example E spotlights a strategy for students to share. Students are asked to think about related facts in the top middle cell. For 7 + 8, students might think about 7 + 7, 8 + 8, or even 10 + 5. During discussion, you can reinforce that these related facts are helpful to students when they can't recall a certain fact. When asked how they think about the fact, students might write 7 + 8 as 7 + 3 + 5 in which they use 10 to find the sum. As with many examples of this routine, this aspect has more than one possible solution. 7 + 8 might also be rewritten 5 + 2. Your discussion with students about these perceptions and strategies bolsters their skillset for recalling facts and working with the operations in general.

E

A Number Bio for 7 + 8

Way to think about it	Two related facts	A way to rewrite It
What it looks like?	Related subtraction facts	Another idea I have

F. Multi-digit multiplication begins in fourth grade for many students. Students learn about how to represent it with arrays and area models and how they can use the distributive property and partial products. These different ideas are included in Example F of *Number Bio*. The example also calls your attention to other useful ideas about the expression. In the upper right cell, students are asked to estimate the product. Some may record that it is about 140 citing 20 × 7 while others might propose that it is about 160 referencing 16 × 10. Again, you have opportunities for rich discussion about diverse perspectives and flexible thinking all accessible through a routine. As with other examples of the routine, you can change the number of conditions and the type of prompts to meet the needs of your class, the topic, or your time frame. However, you might need to limit the number of conditions as computations or numbers become more complex. Or, you might choose to have the prompts completed over two days of the routine.

F

A Number Bio for 16 × 7

It's more than	It's less than	It's about
One way to break it apart	Another way to break it apart	Related expression

NUMBER BIO VARIATION—FRACTIONS

Fractions are numbers. Students need opportunities to think and reason about fractions just as they do with whole numbers. Most, if not all, jump-start routines can be modified to build fraction sense. *Number Bio* is one of them.

G. Example G has students think about $\frac{5}{8}$ in a collection of ways. Those ways are similar to questions asked about whole numbers. In Example B, students thought about which benchmarks 77 was closest to. Here, they consider what benchmark $\frac{5}{8}$ is close to. Students can be asked to represent the fraction with a set or region model. However, it is important that they wrestle with $\frac{5}{8}$ as a number and in the ways that they have thought about whole numbers. $\frac{5}{8}$ might be decomposed into $\frac{1}{8}+\frac{4}{8}$, $\frac{1}{8}+\frac{2}{8}+\frac{2}{8}$, or in a variety of other ways. Those examples can be captured and discussed through the top center and top right cells of the example. Students can be exposed to addition and subtraction of fractions without formal instruction about those operations. In the bottom center cell, students are asked to find $\frac{2}{8}$ more and $\frac{2}{8}$ less, which are examples of addition and subtraction. However, students might find them by putting $\frac{5}{8}$ on a number line and counting forward or backwards by eighths.

G		
A Number Bio for $\frac{5}{8}$		
Is close to 0, $\frac{1}{2}$, or 1	Break it apart	Break apart a different way
How much more for 1 whole? How much more for 2 wholes?	$\frac{2}{8}$ more and $\frac{2}{8}$ less	On a number line

H. Understanding that fractions are numbers is critical. This understanding must also be applied to fractions greater than 1. These fractions can be thought of in the exact same ways as fractions less than 1. In Example H, students work with $\frac{4}{3}$. New ideas about fraction conditions are shown as well. In the upper right cell, students create fractions that are less than the featured fraction. The center cells ask students to represent the fraction with two different models. Asking students to use two different models is intentional as students can develop representational bias of fractions, just like they can with operations and other concepts. Compelling students to represent the same fraction in different ways helps alleviate this bias. Example H also asks students to create their own *feature* about the number.

H		
A Number Bio for $\frac{4}{3}$		
On a number line	A picture of it	Two fractions it is less than
Break it apart	A different picture of it	Create your own idea

CONDITION (FLEXIBLE THINKING)

About the Routine

Games are a great asset in learning mathematics. Games develop strategic thinking, problem solving, and perseverance. Often, games are social endeavors that help students develop behaviors for positively interacting with peers. Yet, there are some students who don't enjoy them. These students might prefer individual investigations, or they may not be very competitive in general. So, for all of the positives about games they can also be a detriment to some students if they are the prime resource for independent work. Most jump-start routines are not designed as games or competitions. This routine, *Condition*, is the outlier. *Condition* is a routine that plays out like a game. In it, students generate a number and record it on a sticky note, index card, or a personal whiteboard. Number conditions are revealed one at a time for students to apply to their number. If their number meets the condition, they earn a point. At the end of a series of conditions, the students with the most points win. Each *game* of condition likely yields multiple winners. For example, a student might generate 63. That student would earn a point if the first condition is that the number is odd. That student would earn a second point if the

next condition is that the number has a 6 in it. Of course, a classmate with the number 46 would also earn a point for the second condition. *Condition* is another take on helping students build capacity with and make connections among the many facets of number. It is similar to *Mystery Number* (Routine 10, page 83) and *Number Bio* (Routine 11, page 87). These ideas are foundations for success in elementary mathematics. Having a collection of routines to reinforce and play with helps you keep the beginning of mathematics interesting and alive.

> Write a three-digit number.
> Match the **CONDITION** to earn a point.
>
> Your number
> • has 5 in it
> • is between 200 and 500
> • rounds to 700
> • has a sum of digits that are even
> • is the smallest three-digit number in the class

Why It Matters

This routine helps students:

- compare and contrast number contexts and conditions;

- reason about various attributes of the same number (MP2);

- observe relationships between different numbers (MP2);

- think flexibly about numbers and concepts;

- consider how to precisely describe numbers (MP6); and

- justify their solutions (MP3).

All tasks can be downloaded for your use at **resources.corwin.com/ jumpstartroutines/elementary**

What They Should Understand First

In *Condition,* students will engage with all sorts of concepts about numbers. They will consider place value and comparison. They will think about one more and one less, two more and two less, even 10 more and 10 less. Ideas about even and odd, rounding, and the results of computation might also be included. Students should have exposure to and instruction with the mathematical concepts presented in the routine. Mastery of any concept is not fully warranted as the concept can be developed and refined through the routine. Another advantage with this routine is that you can limit the conditions to concepts your students have already worked with. Because of this, *Condition* is quite a flexible and useful routine. You can use it any time of the year and it will remain dynamic and relevant.

What to Do

1. Select conditions to use in the routine. Any number of conditions can be used. Be sure to keep the conditions hidden from students.

   [online resources] See downloadable content for a list of possible conditions.

2. Have students generate a number. Students can be prompted to make a number such as *make a two-digit number* or *make a three-digit number.* Another option is to give students number cards or 10-sided dice to generate a number.

3. Reveal a condition to students. Students whose number meets the condition earn a point.

4. Solicit examples of numbers that meet the condition.

5. Reveal the next condition and award points to students with numbers that meet the second condition.

6. Discuss the numbers and conditions as examples are shared. Questions to ask might include:

   » How could your number match more than one condition?

   » Could you rearrange the digits in your number to meet the condition? (for numbers that don't meet the condition)

   » Could you rearrange the digits in your number and still meet the condition? (for numbers that do meet the condition)

   » What are some other numbers that meet this condition that we didn't create?

   » What are some other numbers that would meet each of these conditions that we didn't create?

   » What is the next condition you are hoping for? Why?

7. Adjust the number of conditions as needed to satisfy time considerations and/or student interest and engagement.

8. Celebrate student success.

Anticipated Strategies for This Example

> Write a three-digit number.
> Match the **CONDITION** to earn a point.
>
> Your number
> • has 5 in it
> • is between 200 and 500
> • rounds to 700
> • has a sum of digits that are even
> • is the smallest three-digit number in the class

Students are typically successful with the first prompt in this featured example of *Condition.* However, as you pose new prompts in this example students can be challenged to think about an individual number being able to satisfy more than one of the conditions. This may be evidence of students who see concepts in isolation. This in turn may explain why your students have difficulty retaining information over time. Other things that students might do in this example is create numbers with no zeroes in them.

They might avoid three-digit numbers with the same digit in each place value. As you notice these vacancies in student creations, you can pose new conditions to *nudge* your students toward thinking about *different* numbers. For example, you may find that no student numbers have a 0 in them. The next condition you pose could award a point for a number that has zero tens. And, you might ask it again the next day to get a sense if any students latched on to the thought that a three-digit number can have zero tens. Some conditions in the routine are better suited for reasoning and discussion than others. The third condition in the featured example petitions for numbers that round to 700. Some students will think of numbers between 650 and 699, others will think of numbers between 700 and 749, and others will identify both sets. This is an example of a condition prompt that has potential for rich discussion.

CONDITION—ADDITIONAL EXAMPLES

A. You can use *Condition* with all elementary students, as you can easily modify it for any concept or range of numbers. Example A shows how you might use it in a kindergarten classroom. The two 10 frames captured in the image are available with the slide deck in the downloadable content. You could also choose to have a large double 10 frame on the board that can be manipulated. For young students, you might choose to have them make a model of their number before posing conditions. Conditions themselves can make use of representations. You could alter each condition provided in the example to show the number with a 10 frame or dot card. For example, in the second condition "Is more than 10" you could replace the symbolic number with a representation of 10. The last condition, "Is between 11 and 16 on a number path," is another example of how you can incorporate representations into the routine.

> **A**
>
> Create a number on your ten frames. Match the **CONDITION** to earn a point.
>
> Your number
> - is the smallest number in the class
> - is more than 10
> - is one more than 7
> - is more than 12
> - is two more than 4
> - is between 11 and 16 on a number path

B. Example B builds on the ideas of using representations and tools mentioned in Example A. Here, a 100 chart is provided with the prompts. Students might have their own individual hundred charts or you might post one, large 100 chart to help facilitate discussions. Again, the tool helps students see relationships between numbers and conditions. Each new condition causes a different recording of ideas. Because of this, it might be wise to have two or three large number charts available so that different conditions can be highlighted on a *clean* 100 chart each time. As students begin to work with three-digit numbers, you can use a different collection of 100 charts (e.g., 101–200, 201–300, or 301–400).

> **B**
>
> Choose a number from the hundred chart. Match the **CONDITION** to earn a point.
>
> Your number
> - is more than 20
> - has a 6 in it
> - has 8 ones
> - is close to 100
> - is between 55 and 65
>
> | 1 | 2 | 3 | 4 | 5 | 6 | 7 | 8 | 9 | 10 |
> |---|---|---|---|---|---|---|---|---|----|
> | 11 | 12 | 13 | 14 | 15 | 16 | 17 | 18 | 19 | 20 |
> | 21 | 22 | 23 | 24 | 25 | 26 | 27 | 28 | 29 | 30 |
> | 31 | 32 | 33 | 34 | 35 | 36 | 37 | 38 | 39 | 40 |
> | 41 | 42 | 43 | 44 | 45 | 46 | 47 | 48 | 49 | 50 |
> | 51 | 52 | 53 | 54 | 55 | 56 | 57 | 58 | 59 | 60 |
> | 61 | 62 | 63 | 64 | 65 | 66 | 67 | 68 | 69 | 70 |
> | 71 | 72 | 73 | 74 | 75 | 76 | 77 | 78 | 79 | 80 |
> | 81 | 82 | 83 | 84 | 85 | 86 | 87 | 88 | 89 | 90 |
> | 91 | 92 | 93 | 94 | 95 | 96 | 97 | 98 | 99 | 100 |

C. Collections of basic facts meet conditions as well. Some facts represent doubles. Others are grouped by using tens. There are other ways to think of facts as well. In some cases, both addends or both factors are even. In some cases, the sums and products are even. Some facts have sums greater than 10 while others have sums less than 10. Subtraction and division facts have similar characteristics. Example C shows how you can modify the routine to spotlight ideas about facts. Work with this version of the routine provides a new and different experience to help students grow their understanding of basic facts and basic fact strategies. Using the routine in this way will help your students determine sums and differences when the fact is not automatic for them. It also provides insight that they can apply to other computation situations using larger numbers.

D. Example B alludes to the notion that *Condition* can be used with three-digit numbers. Example D gives that idea better definition by providing examples of what those conditions might be. Some of the conditions in this example, such as the first and fourth, can be applied to two or three-digit numbers. The others will only work with three-digit numbers. Again, there is a condition (rounds to 700) that is likely to elicit rich discussion. Though the first condition is not as rich, it still underscores the idea that many numbers share certain attributes. It calls attention to the idea that some conditions might be better places to begin the routine than others. Thinking about a three-digit number that rounds to 5 is less demanding than thinking about numbers that round to 700. Therefore, it is most likely better to start with the first condition until students have *warmed-up* for the day or to the routine in general. You should also note that not every condition must have multiple solutions. The last condition in this example will have one solution though it is possible that more than one student will have the same number.

C

Write a basic addition fact.
Match the **CONDITION** to earn a point.

Your **addition fact** has a(n)
• sum greater than ten
• doubles fact
• plus one fact
• make ten fact
• even sum
• make ten and some more

D

Write a three-digit number.
Match the **CONDITION** to earn a point.

Your number
• has a 5 in it
• is between 200 and 500
• rounds to 700
• has an even sum of the digits
• is the smallest three-digit number in the class

CONDITION VARIATION—FRACTIONS AND DECIMALS

As mentioned in Part 1, fraction sense can be thought of much like number sense. In fact, fraction sense might be a natural extension, if not part of, our number sense. The same can be said for *decimal sense*. Because of this, you can adjust most every routine to use with fractions or decimals. *Condition* is no different.

E. When we reason about fractions and the results of adding or subtracting with fractions, it is useful to think about how the results compare with certain benchmarks. Is the fraction more or less than $\frac{1}{2}$? Is it close to 0 or 1? Is it more than 1? Students cannot practice with these ideas enough. Fortunately, these are easily folded in as conditions in this routine. You can work in other ideas about equivalency (third condition) and addition (fifth condition) as well. You could even ask if the difference of the generated fraction and 1 is greater than a $\frac{1}{2}$ or a $\frac{1}{3}$.

> **E**
> Write a fraction.
> Match the **CONDITION** to earn a point.
>
> Your fraction
> - is more than $\frac{1}{2}$
> - is equal to $\frac{1}{2}$
> - is equivalent to $\frac{2}{3}$
> - is between 1 and 2
> - can be added to $\frac{3}{4}$ to make one whole

F. Conditions with decimals play out in similar ways as fractions. You can ask students if a decimal is more or less than 0.5 or if it is close to 0 or 1. At first, you might only ask students to generate decimal numbers less than 1. In doing so, the last four conditions in Example F would still work. The first condition would not work. This condition would be best used when you ask students to create a decimal number less than 10 or a decimal number with three digits. In the latter prompt (a decimal with three digits) students might create a number with a digit in the ones, tenths, and hundredths place or a number with a digit in the tens, ones, and tenths place. Again, students might not do this initially. One way you can introduce these *novel* thoughts is for you to also create a number so that something more unique may be considered. Students are likely to run with an idea once they are exposed to it.

> **F**
> Write a decimal number less than 10.
> Match the **CONDITION** to earn a point.
>
> Your decimal
> - is between 5 and 6
> - has a two in it
> - has 8 hundredths
> - has no hundredths
> - has no tenths

CONDITION VARIATION—DIFFERENT ENGAGEMENTS

Condition is ripe for changing the ways your students engage in a routine. Examples G and H describe how that might occur. As with any routine, there is no one right way to use it with your students. You should feel empowered to be flexible and creative. Routines should be an opportunity to engage with thinking about numbers and mathematics in general rather than attempting to replicate an exact way of doing things.

G. *Condition* is a *game routine* in which students create a number and then earn points for satisfying certain conditions. As described so far, one way you can approach this routine is to have your students use their same number for each of the conditions shown in the routine. Another way to engage with the routine would be to have your students use their number for the first condition and then pass their number to a classmate. Then, for the second condition, students have a *new* number to think about. This clever adjustment is applied to Example G. Essentially, there are no new or special conditions that you need to create. This variation will likely cause excitement, laughter, and playful agony. Keep in mind that students should be reminded to pass numbers on so that they don't have a partner's number more than once during the routine.

> ### G
>
> Write a number less than 100.
> Match the **CONDITION** to earn a point.
> **Then pass your number to someone else.**
>
> Your number
> • rounds to 80
> • has a 4 in it
> • is even
> • is the largest number in the class
> • is close to 0

H. Sometimes during class, students need an opportunity to reenergize. This is most likely true after lunch or when mathematics class is at the end of the day. Routines like *Math Yapper* (Routine 1, page 22) are good opportunities to rejuvenate students. A modified version of *Condition* is another way. In Example H, students are asked to stand up if their number meets a condition and sit down if it does not. You can still keep score in this version of *Condition*. However, you might use this version without keeping score and just to get students moving and thinking about numbers.

> ### H
>
> Write a number less than 100.
> Stand up if you meet the **CONDITION.**
> Sit down if you don't meet the **CONDITION.**
>
> Your number
> • has eight ones
> • is larger than 50
> • is between 70 and 90
> • is 20 or more less than your partner

WHERE'S THE POINT? (NUMBER LINE RELATIONSHIPS)

About the Routine

Understanding how numbers are related helps students compare, estimate, and calculate. Seeing relationships between numbers helps them recognize how dynamic number relationships are and helps us make sense of the magnitude of number. Number lines are a useful tool for seeing the relationship between numbers. However, number lines often feature fixed endpoints or specific tick marks that may lead students to think about numbers in limited ways. Such rigidness can inhibit your students' ability to reason about the size of or relationship between numbers. This routine helps students develop a more robust understanding of—and flexible thinking about—numbers and their relationships, which positions them for greater success when working with numbers. This routine presents locations on number lines with limited information about the values those locations might represent. Students then reason about how they can determine what the value might be. They are likely to consider midpoints, quarter-points, and other benchmarks to identify the value. In some situations, like the one presented here,

they may also reason about how the endpoints in a number line change in the same way. The difference between endpoints in this example is 25 so the midpoint must be 25 greater than the first midpoint. Students then share their solutions and reasoning with partners before taking part in a class discussion. At that time, you facilitate a conversation about strategies and reasonable, if not exact, possibilities for the location on the number line.

Where's the Point?

- What number is the arrow pointing to?
- How do you know?

Why It Matters

This routine helps students:

- reason about number relationships using number line models (MP4);

- develop their ideas about half of a number and relationships to other benchmarks (MP2);

- reason about the *closeness* of values. For example, 47 and 54 may be different locations on a number line but they are both *close to* 50 on a number line (MP2);

online resources ↗ All tasks can be downloaded for your use at **resources.corwin.com/ jumpstartroutines/elementary**

- build number sense and confidence for working with numbers;
- think flexibly about quantities and models; and
- defend their reasoning and consider the approaches of others (MP3).

What They Should Understand Before the Routine

In this example of *Where's the Point?*, students find values by reasoning about the relationship between two whole numbers. The first number line has a traditional left endpoint whereas the other endpoints may be quite unusual or unfamiliar. Your students should be aware that endpoints on number lines are not static and that any value rather than the *standard* 0 and 100 or 0 and 1,000 can be used for an endpoint. This routine is intended to refine this understanding as it may not be fully developed. Your students should understand how a number line works and have had some experience with open number lines before working with the routine. They should be able to add and subtract friendly numbers. It will also be helpful if your students are able to reason about numbers that are half of other numbers although they might not be able to find halves fluently and/or with precision. These number lines do not have specific, ticked intervals. Because of this, this routine might be best saved for students in late first grade or early second grade.

What to Do

1. Determine the number of number lines to use in the routine. Note that not all number lines must be discussed during the routine due to time restrictions. Two or three number lines will be sufficient.

2. Present students with one or more number lines with specific endpoints and an arrow pointing to a location on the number line, as in the example provided. Note that it may be desirable to investigate one number line without the other number lines appearing before moving to a second and potentially a third number line.

3. Prompt students to think independently about the relationship between the numbers to determine the value of the unknown location.

4. After finding a value, ask students to share their solutions and reasoning with a partner.

5. Bring students together. Solicit and record various possibilities offered by students.

6. After collecting different possibilities, explore reasoning that justifies those solutions.

7. Have students share their reasoning and ask others to signal if they used a similar strategy.

8. Ask students to share their thinking and probe ideas about how they determined the value of the missing point. Questions to ask might include:
   » How did you find the value of the arrow?
   » What was half of the distance between these values?
   » How did half help you think about the possible solution?
   » Were there other relationships that were helpful?
   » Did anyone think about the number line in a different way?
   » How did you find the value of the second number line?
   » Did anyone begin with the bottom number line before working with the top number line? How was that helpful?

9. Honor and explore both accurate and flawed reasoning.

10. Consider providing students with calculators or 100 charts to help them accurately find values.

11. If time permits, consider extending the routine by creating a new number line with a similar location and a new set of endpoints or ask students to do this.

Anticipated Strategies for This Example

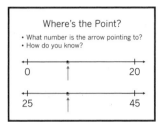

Be prepared for some of your students to identify the value of the arrow as the next counting number from the last known value. In this example, they would share 1 for the top number line and 26 for the second number line. This might hint at students who aren't quite ready for the routine yet. It might also signal that they are not yet thinking about how numbers are related spatially. They might not be thinking about how far from 0 is 20, 25, 50 or 100. You can strengthen their understanding by examining spatial relationships between numbers on number charts. You can also help them make connections between number charts and number lines during discussion. Students might use another strategy by picking a *halfway* number each time that an arrow is between two numbers regardless how close the arrow is to the middle of those numbers. Students might also choose numbers at random without any reasoning or justification about their selections. This should improve as experience with the routine is gained. It may be helpful to give landmarks on the number line to improve student accuracy with the routine. Here, you might offer where 10 and 35 are on each number line or where 5 and 30 or 15 and 40 are.

WHERE'S THE POINT?—ADDITIONAL EXAMPLES

A. *Where's the Point?* can take advantage of different relationships on a number line. Two adjacent number lines can focus students on similar changes to the endpoints of a number line. In Example A, the top and middle number lines have endpoints that have changed by 200. Therefore, the value of the arrow should change by 200. The middle and bottom number lines play on the concept of the interval between endpoints. In this same example, the endpoints on each number line are 110 apart. The arrow is the same distance from each endpoint on both number lines so the value might be 20 or so more than the left endpoint. Keep in mind that these three number lines are shown together for convenience. The two distinct ideas (same change in the top/middle number lines and same interval in the middle/bottom number lines) that they represent would be best reserved for separate days.

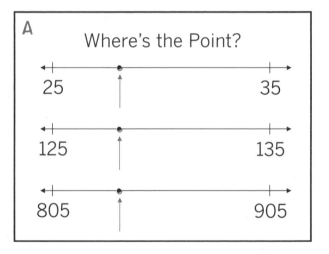

B. As your students' reasoning about relationships grows, you can begin to shift the placement of the unknowns. You may continue to highlight benchmark locations such as midpoints as shown in the last number line in Example B. The location can also be shifted more dramatically. The top number line shows an interval of 20. It might be especially challenging for students to think of numbers so close to 50 (40 and 60) as also being far apart. Students might determine that the marked location on the top number line is 58. Others might suggest 57 or 56. You should accept reasonable answers. Strategies should be discussed and explored. In this example, students are likely to find some way to quantify the space in between. Some may think about 50 as the midpoint and then partition the remaining distance in some way. Others may attempt to partition the entire space between 40 and 60.

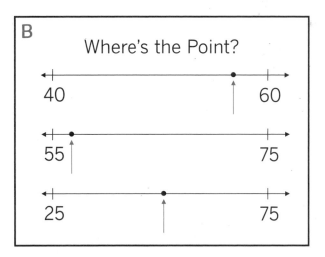

C. For some students, visual references to benchmark locations may be needed to support their reasoning. This version might actually be the place to begin for many students. It provides tick marks to help them make sense of the distance between numbers. These tick marks can support counting intervals as well as hold the location of certain numbers for students as they determine the possible value of the noted point. The number of and interval of tick marks should be based on the needs of students. In time, tick marks should be lessened and removed altogether.

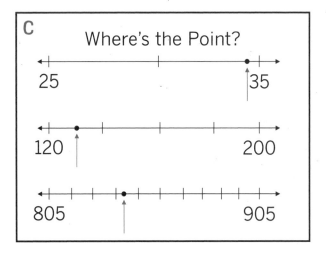

It might be wise to begin with traditional endpoints on number lines be they 0 and 100, 0 and 1,000, or something similar. You can nurture better developed strategies that can be applied to more unusual number lines by beginning with these endpoints. You can also help students see relationships more clearly by using related number lines in the same routine. For example, one number line can have endpoints of 0 and 100 and the other can have related endpoints such as 200 and 300. Example C shows a different strategy for supporting students.

D. Later in elementary school, *Where's the Point?* can be modified to bolster student understanding of fractions. When working with fractions, students often experience similarly stagnate endpoints of 0 and 1. This may be a necessary starting point. However, your students should be moved to reason about other possibilities as well. In Example D, students first think about a location between 0 and 1. They might find it to be $\frac{1}{3}$ or $\frac{1}{4}$. The next two number lines show a targeted value in the exact same location as the first number line. Yet, these number lines have different endpoints. The endpoints of the middle number line are one more than those of the top therefore the arrow is one more or $1\frac{1}{3}$ or $1\frac{1}{4}$. The endpoints of the bottom number line can be thought of in a similar way creating a similar justification for the arrow's value to be $7\frac{1}{3}$ or $7\frac{1}{4}$. This version of *Where's the Point?* is a good opportunity for you to help students see how fractions are related and that the distance between any two consecutive whole numbers can be thought of in similar ways.

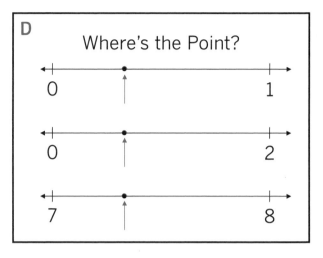

NOTES

WHERE'S THE POINT?
VARIATION—BASE 10 RELATIONSHIPS

Numbers and number relationships can become more and more challenging to think about as the number of place values increase. Essentially, it can be hard to think about very big and very small numbers (Krasa & Shunkwiler, 2009). Students learn about powers of 10 in later grades but the understanding of the concept may not be fully realized at first. *Where's the Point?* can help your students see relationships between *similar* numbers sooner and in turn serve as a foundation for work with powers of 10.

E. Example E shows how powers of 10 can be applied to *Where's the Point?* Here, the first number line shows a distance of 100. Many fourth and fifth graders will be able to easily determine the location to be about 310 or 320. The next number line has endpoints that are 10 times greater than the first number line. In fact, 300 and 400 would not even appear on this second number line. The location of the point has not moved so that point is 10 times more than the one just above it. 3,100 or 3,200 would be reasonable. You might discuss the midpoints of each number line as well. In fact, these might be the starting places for students' reasoning rather than thinking about 10 times more. The bottom number line is 10 times more than the middle. The value of the point noted by the arrow can be found in a similar way. It can be thought of as being 31,000 or 32,000. The potential of the routine is clear in this instance. Yet, you might start this example with endpoints of 30 and 40 before moving to larger numbers to better support your students.

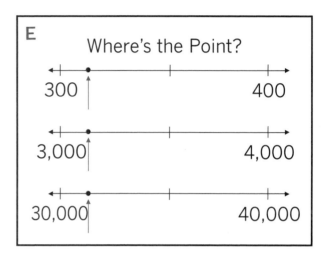

F. Example F builds on the idea of powers of 10. However, it reverses how the numbers change. Finding a tenth of a number might be quite the challenge for students. You can adjust the routine so that all number lines are provided at the same time.

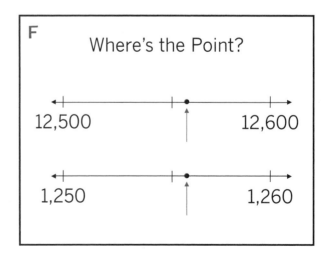

WHERE'S THE POINT? VARIATION—SHIFTING POINTS

Where's the Point? can build other ideas about number and number relationships through careful manipulation of the number lines and endpoints.

G. Points on a number line change in various ways. Two seemingly identical locations will have different values due to other known points. This routine has made use of endpoints but other locations can be just as useful. These manipulations can be fodder for some enthusiastic debates about the value of unknown locations. Example G shows how you can shift the points on a number line and how endpoints can be marked with unknown values. You might withhold these variations of *Where's the Point?* until after your students have had quite a bit of time working with and reasoning about values on empty number lines.

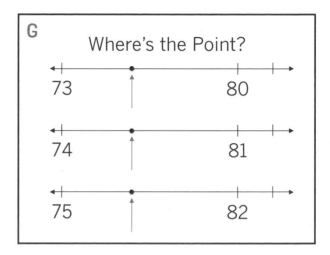

H. Example H offers one last variation for the routine. Here, the right endpoints in each number line are the same as is the position of the arrow on each number line. If Example G didn't ignite debate Example H is sure to do so. Your students might attempt to simply adjust each value by adding 50 to each new number line. In fact, many students will insist that *is* how one must find the unknown values. Others might argue that the space between the endpoints is being *squished* resulting in a changed value of the arrow but not a change of 50. Arguments from both sides will offer great insight into student thinking.

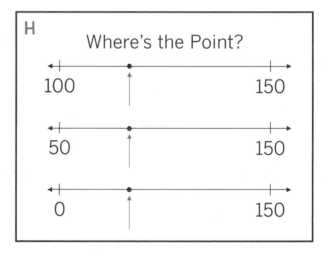

IS THIS THE END? (NUMBER LINE RELATIONSHIPS)

About the Routine

Understanding how numbers relate to one another is a hallmark of number sense. Refined understanding of number relationships is evident when we recognize that any number has an infinite variety of relationships. This understanding enables us to think flexibly about numbers as well as strategies to derive efficient approaches to computation. Yet, dynamic relationships between numbers can be compromised by the static use of number lines. *Is This the End?* is a routine that uses a number line representation to develop student thinking and reasoning about numbers and number relationships. In this routine, students consider possible endpoints for a number line with a given point which at first is the midpoint. This routine is unique because typically students identify points on a number line when given endpoints. In fact, those endpoints are often stagnant featuring numbers like 0 and 1, 0 and 100, 0 and 1,000, and so on. In this routine, students are given a value for a place on a number line. With that information, students determine viable options for each endpoint. As students share their ideas with classmates, they are exposed to

> The arrow is pointing at 345.
> What are the endpoints?

different, logical possibilities. This discussion in turn helps students consider how numbers are related to a variety of other numbers and how they can justify those relationships. In time, the location of the unknown value can shift from the midpoint to other places on the number line. You might also consider modifying the routine to ask students to find more than one set of endpoints for the same number at the same location.

Why It Matters

This routine helps students:

- consider how a number relates to another number (MP2);

- reason about how two numbers relate to a third (MP2);

- develop a sense of relative position and relationship (as the location changes);

- look for and manipulate patterns and structure within relationships (MP8);

 All tasks can be downloaded for your use at **resources.corwin.com/ jumpstartroutines/elementary**

- reinforce ideas about friendly numbers or benchmarks;
- develop confidence with quantity and computation;

- communicate their reasoning with others (MP3); and
- listen actively to the reasoning of others (MP3).

What They Should Understand First

Students should demonstrate understanding of number lines with tick marks before working with open number lines as presented in this routine. Their work with ticked number lines should also feature shifting or changing endpoints as well. This might include a ticked number line with end points of 10 and 20 or 25 and 75 in first grade. This also exposes students to the notion that the location of any number can change based on the position of other numbers on the number line. Your students do not need to be fluent skip-counters or capable of finding half with ease. However, work with skip-counting prior to work with this routine may be useful. Understanding one-more/one-less, two-more/two-less, and 10-more/10-less is essential. Ideas about other more/less situations such as five-more/five-less may be helpful but aren't necessary.

What to Do

1. Draw or project a number line on the board with a *known* location and unknown endpoints. Early experiences should present the known as the midpoint. Also note that it should be clearly stated that it is the midpoint or middle of the two values.

2. Give students a value that represents the known location on the number line.

3. Ask students to determine what the endpoints might be for the number line based on the value of the known location. First exposure to the routine can be supported with printed number lines or student journals. In time, the routine can become a mental activity.

4. Note: After some exposure, students can be prompted to find more than one set of possible endpoints. Teachers may consider challenging the class to find a given number of sets of endpoints as a class challenge.

5. Have students share their endpoints with classmates in small groups or with partners.

6. Bring the class together. Ask students to share sets of endpoints. Record the sets of endpoints that students share. Record multiple responses before discussing accuracy and reasoning.

7. After student ideas are collected, discuss the solutions offered by the class.

8. Honor and explore both accurate and flawed reasoning. Highlight how endpoints are related to the midpoint and possible relationships between sets of endpoints. Questions to ask might include:

    » How did you find your endpoints?

    » How do you know the endpoints are accurate?

    » Are there any sets of endpoints that are similar? How are they similar?

    » Are there any endpoints that you find surprising?

    » Do you notice any patterns in the endpoints that we created as a class?

    » Is there any set of endpoints that were shared that you are unsure of or that you would like to argue?

    » What is a strategy you might use next time? Why?

9. Consider offering a set of endpoints with an unusual interval and asking students if this new set is possible and why.

Anticipated Strategies for This Example

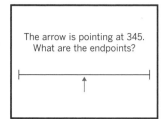

The arrow is pointing at 345. What are the endpoints?

For many of us, the strategy for finding the endpoints of a number line with 345 in the middle (the featured example) is to double 345. It enables us to create endpoints of 0 and something (690). This strategy, though viable, shows the deeply ingrained idea that number lines must have endpoints of 0 and something. Although we know that there are infinite possibilities, we rely on this approach. Students are likely to do the same though they might double by adding the given number to itself (345 + 345). It's possible that they recognize and know other possibilities. Some students will. They may think of one-more and one-less to create endpoints of 344 and 346 for this example. Others will use two-more and two-less while others will use 10-more and 10-less. Students may find incorrect endpoints due to calculation or counting errors. This is more likely to occur with *irregular* intervals such as nine-more and nine-less or 27-more and 27-less. You should look for students who consistently apply the same strategy (e.g., one-more/one-less) and in time restrict that as a possibility in order to advance student thinking.

IS THIS THE END?—ADDITIONAL EXAMPLES

A. Using 345 as the midpoint is not an option for some students, like kindergarteners or first graders, who haven't been introduced to numbers greater than 100 or 120. But, those students can still think about how numbers are related and how the tools and representations used in mathematics show relationships between numbers. In Example A, students are presented with 13 as the midpoint of the number line. They might find 12 and 14 as endpoints. Some might find 11 and 15 and others might even find 3 and 23. The symbolic representation of 13 could be changed to a double 10 frame. These young mathematicians could have personal double 10 frames to manipulate in order to find more and less of 13. Using this version at this level boosts other skills and concepts, including counting forward and backward, addition and subtraction, and more or less. Students who use visuals with the routine, like 10 frames, should connect them to the symbolic numbers. You can do this for them when appropriate.

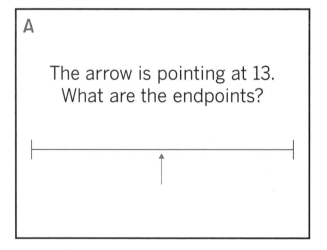

A

The arrow is pointing at 13. What are the endpoints?

B. The featured example of 345 likely works well in second grade and early third grade. It is natural to extend their deepening understanding of numbers and number relationships to four-digit numbers before working with even larger numbers such as five- and six-digit numbers. Example B posts a four-digit number in the routine. Also note that the number 2,836 is less friendly. Simply, 2,836 might be more challenging for students to think about relationally than 2,500, 2,750, or 2,800 for example. Before you move students to four-digit numbers, you should see balanced success with three-digit numbers. Students should work well with benchmark-type numbers of 345, 750, and 800 and equally well with numbers like 337, 761, and 814 before working with four-digit numbers.

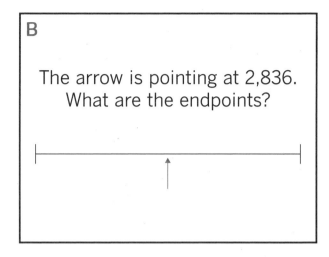

C. Throughout this book, the argument has been made that fractions are numbers and sense of fractions is part of having number sense. Many variations of jump-start routines suggest how fractions can be featured. Example C of *Is This the End?* shows you how fractions can serve as values for midpoints of a number line. Strategies for finding endpoints of whole numbers should be transferred to fractions and mixed numbers like $2\frac{6}{8}$. Unit fractions can be used to find endpoints of $2\frac{5}{8}$ and $2\frac{7}{8}$. An interval of one whole can be used to argue endpoints of $1\frac{6}{8}$ and $3\frac{6}{8}$. Students might even add and subtract $\frac{6}{8}$ from the midpoint establishing 2 and $3\frac{4}{8}$ as their endpoints. These strategies for finding endpoints with fractions may seem simplistic. But, it is understanding that most fourth and fifth grade teachers would gladly welcome.

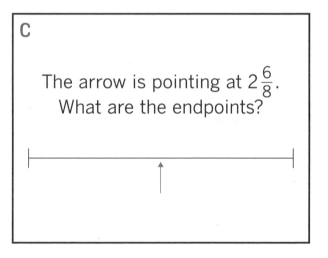

D. A number is halfway between two other numbers. But, it can also be closer to a certain number than another. Example D has students begin to think about relationships and proximity. In this example, students cannot be as precise as in other examples of the routine. Here, 48 is positioned close to the right endpoint. Even so, some students might believe the endpoints to be 47 and 49. This is evidence of an overgeneralized misconception that all of the space between two endpoints is noted by a number. This might occur for a variety of reasons, including experiences with number paths, observations of ticked number lines, or previous experience with this routine in which the midpoint was always used. Students who are challenged by this variation should have access to number charts and other tools to help them make sense of the relationships. You should accept a variety of solutions that are reasonable for this variation. In this example, endpoints of 39 and 49 would be reasonable if the distance between the endpoints is 20. But, endpoints of 29 and 49 are also reasonable if the distance is 20. Of course, it could also be argued that the endpoints are 30 and 50.

D
The arrow is pointing at 48. What are the endpoints?

NOTES

_____

_____

_____

_____

_____

_____

_____

_____

_____

_____

_____

_____

_____

IS THIS THE END? VARIATION—DIFFERENT KNOWNS

One location was given in the previous examples. You can take another approach to the routine as well. You could ask students to find locations other than endpoints. Or, you might provide an endpoint and a known location and ask students to place other numbers on the number line.

E. Clearly, Example E is quite different than the other examples of the routine. But, the thinking and reasoning remains the same. Students still have to think about how numbers are related to one another. In fact, it still makes use of a midpoint. As noted in the directions, it is fine for you to tell students that the arrow/value is exactly in the middle of the number line. In this example, knowing that the middle is 20 other relationships have to be considered. What would the right endpoint be? Are all of the options presented (10, 22, and 45) possibilities for this number line as drawn? 45 isn't on this number line as drawn. It would be just past the right endpoint. It would also be acceptable for students to extend the number line to justify where 45 should be placed.

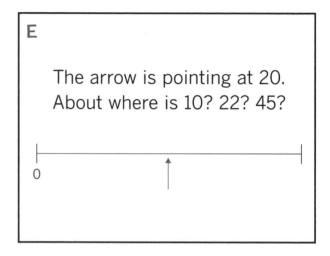

F. A criticism of number line use is that the endpoints are often stagnant and rely on a left endpoint of 0. This is not to say those endpoints should never be used. They are helpful, and so Example E shows how you might use them with this variation of the routine. Keep in mind that this variation of the routine could also have any value for the left endpoint. Here, 400 is the left endpoint, and 500 is the midpoint. Students are asked to place different numbers on the number line. After they do so, you might consider shifting the location of 500 and asking them how the locations of the other numbers would also shift.

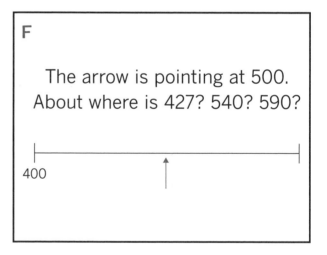

IS THIS THE END? VARIATION—COMPUTATION AND BASIC FACTS

Relational understanding is a good way to acquire and recall basic facts. It is an underpinning of other computational strategies, including partials and compensations. The midpoint of this routine can be any whole number, fraction, or decimal. But, the midpoint could also be an expression.

G. Knowing 3 + 7 = 10 can help students find 13 + 7. Thinking about 13 + 7 as 10 more than 3 + 7 and 10 less than 23 + 7 could also be helpful. And, you can highlight these ideas through the routine. There are other patterns that could be established through the routine as well. Knowing 13 + 7 also helps students find other sums. For example, they can surmise that 12 + 7 is one less than 20 and that 14 + 7 is one more than 20. It can be reasoned that 13 + 6 is one less and that 13 + 8 is one more than 13 + 7. It is clear that this level of understanding is both deep and robust. It enables students to refine strategies and develop computational fluency. All of which can begin with or be supported by *Is This the End?*

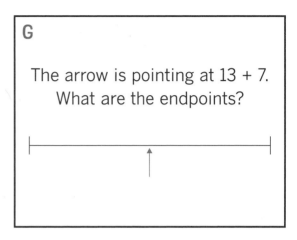

G

The arrow is pointing at 13 + 7.
What are the endpoints?

H. Students are expected to understand that changing factors changes products. They use this understanding to find 8 × 6 by knowing that it is one more group of 8 than 8 × 5. Though explored with arrays and equal groups, the idea isn't always well understood or applied. This routine might be an opportunity to practice and reinforce the concept. Here, 7 × 5 is the midpoint of the number line. Therefore, 7 × 4 and 7 × 6 could be endpoints. Of course, 7 × 3 and 7 × 7, 7 × 1 and 7 × 9 could also be endpoints. The first factor could be manipulated instead resulting in endpoints of 6 × 5 and 8 × 5 or 5 × 5 and 9 × 5. Reasoning and discussion might include the products but it doesn't necessarily have to. The products themselves may be discussed *after* endpoints are established. As with anything, you might provide fact charts as needed to support student accuracy.

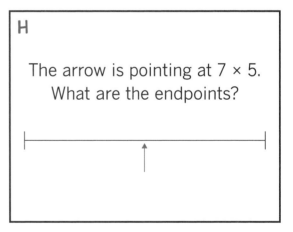

H

The arrow is pointing at 7 × 5.
What are the endpoints?

ABOUT OR BETWEEN (ESTIMATING RESULTS)

About the Routine

Students often apply rules and procedures to mathematics with fragile understanding of or unfinished learning about certain skills or concepts. Their use of algorithms can lead to bizarre results. For example, when first learning about the addition algorithm, they may regroup every place value if it is warranted or not. Sometimes, place value of digits is overlooked—even ignored—when carrying out the multiplication or division algorithms. What's worse is that students are unable to recognize that their results are way off. The understanding about number relationships, place value, and operations that they showed once does not transfer to these new procedures. Unfortunately, the inability to determine the reasonableness of calculations *does* transfer to other topics, including word problems and other problem-solving situations. One approach to counter these difficulties is to have students estimate results often, if not every time they compute, and then compare their actual results to the predicted results or estimations. But, skilled estimation takes time and practice. It takes experience. It relies on a diverse portfolio of strategies that extend beyond rounding alone. It includes using friendly or compatible numbers. It

About or Between
39 + 47
87 + 35
19 + 66

also makes use of thinking about a range for the exact solution. This routine, *About or Between*, is an opportunity for students to gain experience with estimating. More importantly, students are exposed to the estimation strategies and reasoning of others so that they can grow their skillset. In the routine, students are presented with one or more expressions. They are charged with estimating to find an *about* answer or to find a range that the actual result will fall *between*. You can modify the routine to prompt for only *about* ideas or *between* ideas.

Why It Matters

This routine helps students:

- practice estimating sums, differences, products, or quotients to determine if calculations are reasonable (MP2);

- determine if using a range is better for estimating a solution to determine reasonableness (MP2);

- justify their estimated results (MP3);

online resources ↖ All tasks can be downloaded for your use at **resources.corwin.com/ jumpstartroutines/elementary**

- consider strategies used by other students (MP3);
- improve the precision of their estimated sums, differences, products, or quotients (MP6); and
- reinforce ideas about friendly numbers or benchmarks.

What They Should Understand First

About or Between should be preceded with explicit instruction about estimation and estimation strategies. Students should show understanding and recognition of compatible numbers and benchmarks. Evidence of this understanding may appear in other routines. Students will need to be able to operate with compatible and friendly numbers but do not have to show fluency with them. You might remove the *between* aspect of this routine at first so that the routine only focuses on *about*. However, students of all ages are able to think about a number that is too high and a number that is too low for given situations. In fact, this is a clever slant on the estimating and counting experience in *Picture It* (Routine 5, page 48). Even so, estimating a range for an operation is a bit more complex. To find the range for a sum, we would add two *lesser* compatible numbers and two *greater* compatible numbers. Of course, a range could be found by adjusting just one of the addends in a similar way.

What to Do

1. Create one or more expressions for students to work with. Note that initially it may be best to use only one expression. Also note that when more than one expression is written it may be wise to pose one at a time.

2. Have students estimate the sum, difference, product, or quotient. Or, have students find a range for the exact result to fall in.

3. Have students share their estimates and strategies with a partner.

4. Solicit and record estimates and/or ranges for the expression. Multiple, reasonable, estimated results are possible. This can be difficult for students to accept.

5. Bring the class back together to discuss strategies for finding estimates efficiently. Be mindful that some strategies may not be efficient or strategies at all. Questions to ask might include:
   - » How are the estimates related?
   - » What strategy did you use to find your estimate?
   - » How was your strategy efficient for you?
   - » How did your estimate compare to others?
   - » How could there be more than one estimated solution?
   - » Why did you choose to find a range instead of finding an *about* estimate?
   - » How did you find your range?
   - » How do the estimates compare to the range?
   - » How precise were the estimates?

6. Consider inserting a strategy that students don't offer. This may be likely for finding a range. Note that sharing ideas about a range can be done without explicit instruction during the routine. Also note that the concept of a range might be acquired through frequent, consistent exposure during this addition by the teacher after the routine.

7. Reinforce to students that there is not a *best* strategy for estimating. This may also include recognition that a certain strategy may be easier to use but less precise.

8. Honor all contributions and thinking.

Anticipated Strategies for This Example

About or Between

39 + 47

87 + 35

19 + 66

Sometimes rounding numbers is perfect for estimating, and the estimated result is the exact same as finding compatible numbers or benchmarks. Sometimes rounding isn't as precise. For example, the rounded estimate of 24 + 24 is 40 whereas the *compatible estimate* of 25 + 25 is more precise. Students can estimate by thinking about *close to* before formal introduction of rounding. In the featured example, 39 + 47 might be thought of as 40 + 50. Students without exposure to rounding can still consider it in this way. The range for this expression is between 70 and 90 found with 30 + 40 and 40 + 50. Other possibilities for the range include between 79 and 89 and between 77 and 87. In each of these, one addend remains unchanged when finding the range and the other is adjusted to the next greater friendly and the next lesser friendly. It is important for you to *take stock* of student preferences for certain strategies during the routine. You can begin to insert new strategies or approaches if students seem to favor one or another. Though no one strategy is best for estimating results, students should have different strategies to use as numbers and operations change.

ABOUT OR BETWEEN—ADDITIONAL EXAMPLES

A. If not careful, routines can inadvertently feature one operation over another. This is also true for the type and size of numbers used in routines. Example A is a reminder that *About or Between* works perfectly well with subtraction. The *about* difference of 51 – 17 might be thought of as 50 – 20, 51 – 20, and even 50 – 25. Finding a range with subtraction can pose a greater challenge. To do so, the minuend and the subtrahend in *opposite* have to be adjusted in opposite directions. For example, to find the range of 89 – 33 we would use 80 – 40 and 90 – 30 creating a range for the difference to be between 40 and 60. This can be rather complicated and inefficient. Adjusting only the minuend or the subtrahend might be better. For 89 – 33, a range could be generated by finding the differences of 89 – 30 and 89 – 40 or by finding the differences of 80 – 33 and 90 – 33. Clearly, adjusting the subtrahend is likely the better option for estimating.

A

About or Between

51 – 17

89 – 33

64 – 26

B. Adding or subtracting three- and four-digit numbers is more likely to yield errors as the procedures become a bit more complex. Estimating becomes even more useful in these cases. Yet, the strategies for estimating results remain unchanged. In Example B, students estimate the sums of three-digit addends. The sum of the 489 + 77 is an example of a calculation that might go haywire. But, the estimated or *about* sum can be found in similar ways as two-digit addends. Students might think of it as about 580 by rounding both addends. Ranges are useful here, too. The sum of 489 + 77 falls between 400 + 70 and 500 + 80. Of course, there are other range possibilities as well. For example, students could find the range as between 400 + 0 and 500 + 100. Again, students might adjust only one addend. Though either can be adjusted, you can facilitate discussions about why it makes more sense to manipulate 489 rather than 77.

B

About or Between

158 + 301

489 + 77

640 + 275

C. Estimating products of multi-digit factors is a good modification of the routine. Example C shows what *About and Between* might look like in these cases. You might use the example in fourth grade just after students have started working with two-digit by one-digit multiplication. You might bring it out again later in the year. It could be used in fifth grade, too. The product of 14 × 7 is about 70 (10 × 7). Some students might argue that it is 140 (14 × 10). The debriefing discussion can then *dig into* which estimate (and related strategy) might be better. The second expression, 38 × 5, presents a different conversation in that students might find their estimates by thinking of 40 × 5 while others think of *about half* of 380 or 38 × 10. Ranges for products are also worthwhile pursuits. Even so, some expressions like 61 × 6 might lend themselves better to *about* products rather than ranges.

C

About or Between

14 × 7

38 × 5

61 × 6

D. You can extend estimation strategies to expressions with two multi-digit factors. In Example D, the product of 31×28 might be reasoned to be about 900 as both factors can be rounded to 30. But if both factors are rounded in the second expression, the product would be quite different than the actual product. This is another case for students to have multiple, flexible estimation strategies. Estimating 15×17 to be about 15×20 works quite well. Thinking of 17 as 18 so that doubling and halving can be leveraged is also quite crafty. Doing so, changes 15×17 to 15×18, which can then be thought of as 30×9 or 270. So, a student can present 15×17 as about 270. Finding the range of products is similar to finding the range of sums. The third expression 84×77 (6,468) is between 80×70 (5,600) and 90×80 (7,200).

D

About or Between

31×28

15×17

84×77

NOTES

ABOUT OR BETWEEN VARIATION—DIVISION

For one reason or another, division often seems left behind in classroom games, centers, and routines. It may be that playing or working with division is just not as easy to think about. It might be that student challenges with other operations divert time and attention from division. Like other routines, *About or Between* is the perfect opportunity to play with division. After all, estimating quotients is incredibly necessary as any approach to division, from partial quotients to the standard algorithm, often goes awry.

E. You can take advantage of *About and Between* soon after learning about division with multi-digit dividends. You might introduce a division version, as shown in Example E, only a day or two after the concept is introduced. The routine may help students become proficient with the skills and concepts inherent in multi-digit division more quickly as it reinforces thinking and reasoning needed for carrying out division procedures. For the first example, students may think that $74 \div 6$ is about 10 ($60 \div 6$). Some may suggest 11, 12, or even 15 recognizing that 74 is a bit more than 60 so the quotient will a bit more than 10 as well. Some students might adjust the divisor instead. In $74 \div 6$, students might estimate the quotient to be about 10 because $74 \div 7$ is about 10.

E

About or Between

$74 \div 6$

$155 \div 7$

$98 \div 3$

F. A range or *the between* is a useful strategy for division as well. It is applied in similar ways. Students have the option of adjusting the dividend to two different friendly or compatible numbers. In some cases, the divisor might be adjusted and in others both are adjusted. The range of the second expression in Example F can be thought of as between $700 \div 50$ and $800 \div 50$. As with other examples of the routine, the discussion that occurs afterward is critical for advancing your students' understanding.

F

About or Between

$278 \div 25$

$714 \div 51$

$1,206 \div 83$

ABOUT OR BETWEEN VARIATION—FRACTIONS

Computing fractions can be as perplexing as multi-digit division. Finding common denominators, converting mixed numbers, and other procedures can be easily muddled. Estimating results of computing fractions is tremendously helpful especially when confronting unlike denominators. Estimating results of like denominators is a possibility for the routine. But, doing so is less practical as addition and subtraction of like denominators is less demanding. Also notice that *between* may be less practical in some of these examples so the routine might become only *about*.

G. Before students can estimate results of adding or subtracting fractions, they must first show solid understanding of benchmark fractions and flexible comparison strategies. They should easily recognize that $\frac{1}{8}$ is close to 0 and that $\frac{4}{5}$ is close to 1. They will apply these ideas to *About or Between*. For the first expression in Example G, students might estimate the difference to be about $\frac{1}{2}$ or even a little less than $\frac{1}{2}$. This proposition is grounded in $\frac{8}{10}$ being close to 1 and $\frac{2}{4}$ being equal to $\frac{1}{2}$. For the right expression, students might advocate that the sum is about six as the sum of 3 and 2 is 5 and the fractional parts add up to about one more whole.

G

| About |

$$\frac{8}{10} - \frac{2}{4} = \qquad 3\frac{4}{6} + \frac{1}{3} + 2\frac{1}{3}$$

H. Multiplication and division with fractions are both practical applications of the routine in late fourth grade, fifth grade, and even into middle school. In Example H, students might reason that the product of the first expression is about 24. Others might believe it to be about 25 by thinking that 6×4 is 24 and that 6 more halves will be about 3 more. Thinking about a range becomes once again useful for multiplying and dividing fractions. For example, $6 \times 4\frac{1}{2}$ will be between 6×4 and 6×5 because $4\frac{1}{2}$ is between 4 and 5. In the second expression, students think about how many $2\frac{1}{4}$s are in 10. They might reason that it will be about 5 relying on the basic fact $10 \div 2$. Others might suggest it is less than 5 as they consider the effect of the divisor being more than two. As with division of whole numbers, finding the range is likely easier found by adjusting only the dividend of the divisor.

H

| About |

$$6 \times 4\frac{1}{2} = \qquad 10 \div 2\frac{1}{4}$$

MORE OR LESS (ESTIMATING RESULTS)

About the Routine

"Is my answer reasonable?" We want our students to ask themselves this question nearly every time they work with a problem or calculation. Yet, many of our students don't often consider if their answer is reasonable. They engage in mathematics mechanically. They blindly rely on procedures, pencils, or calculators to find solutions. Because of this, they may make computation errors or enter the wrong numbers on a calculator having no idea that their result is impossible or wildly inaccurate. Is 27 + 26 greater than 50? Of course, the numbers could be lined up to use the algorithm. The addends could be decomposed to add tens and ones. Some students might count on from 27 by 26 ones to determine their solution. In some cases, students will reason that 25 + 25 = 50 and because both addends are greater the sum must also be greater. So, is 29 + 19 more than 50? How do we know? How does knowing help? These are the questions at the center of this routine, *More or Less*. In it, students estimate sums, differences, products, and quotients. They compare their estimates to

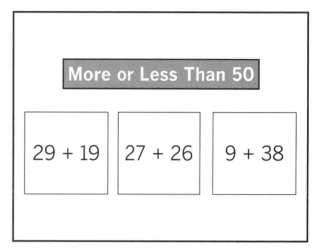

a posted number, which is often a benchmark number. They justify how they estimated the result and how it compares to the given value. This routine is intended to be a mental math activity. So, all desks should be clear of pencils, paper, and other tools for finding exact answers. The routine also plays well when students are called to the carpet in lieu of working at their desks.

Why It Matters

This routine helps students:

- estimate sums, differences, products, and quotients (MP2);

- ask themselves if an answer is reasonable (MP6);

- determine efficient strategies for computing (MP2);

- consider when and if a calculation tool is needed (MP5);

- compare estimates with actual results;

- identify if their computations are accurate (MP6); and

- defend their reasoning and consider the strategies of others (MP3).

 All tasks can be downloaded for your use at **resources.corwin.com/ jumpstartroutines/elementary**

What They Should Understand First

Before working with the featured example of this routine, your students should have a firm grasp of the meaning of addition. They should be able to represent addition in a variety of ways and make use of number lines or number charts, which will come in handy when making arguments about their reasoning. For this late first or early second grade example, students should also have learned about adding two-digit numbers, which is built on understanding of place value. In previous lessons, students should have some exposure to prompts that have them look for patterns within expressions or ask them to estimate results before adding. As with all other jump-start routines, students do not need to show mastery of basic facts to work with this routine. Practice and discussion of *More or Less* should have a tangential effect on student fact acquisition.

What to Do

1. Present two or three expressions for students and a number to compare results with. Note that the number of expressions can be limited or expanded relative to student proficiency and time allocations. Also note that it may be best to offer one expression for consideration and discussion at a time.

2. Have students decide how the results of the expression(s) compare to a given value. As noted, this is a mental mathematics opportunity. Students should not use tools to find exact values.

3. Provide time for students to reason about the expression(s).

4. Have students share their ideas with a partner before having a whole class discussion.

5. Begin the whole-class discussion, by identifying who believed that the expression was more or less than the target.

6. Ask students to share how they made their decisions. As students share their thinking, it is important that we probe thinking and ask clarifying questions rather than ask questions to establish how we thought about the expression. Questions might include:

   » How did you estimate your solution?

   » Why did you think about the numbers in those ways?

   » How were those numbers easier or more useful to work with?

   » How did your estimated sum compare to the given value?

   » Might there have been a better or more precise estimate?

   » Could you think about your solution using a different operation?

   » How does your thinking compare to (another student's)?

   » How are the different strategies similar?

   » What is a strategy you might use next time? Why?

7. Honor and explore both accurate and flawed reasoning.

8. Consider providing exact values after discussion so that students can compare and confirm their more or less estimates.

Anticipated Strategies for This Example

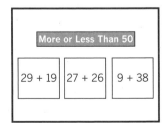

It is entirely possible, if not somewhat likely, that some students will attempt to use a procedure to find the sums and then compare them to 50 (prompted comparison in the featured example). This may occur even if algorithms haven't been taught in school. Some students might describe thinking about base 10 blocks in their heads or using a mental number line. While possible, this imagining of physical representations and number lines may prove to be problematic as numbers become more complex. From time to time, students offer this *strategy* as another idea when it is not necessarily something they even did. You should acknowledge the strategy but also be careful not to inadvertently favor it more or overemphasize it. Strategies of partial sums, adjusting, and compensation might be offered. You should also listen for comparison strategies grounded in reasoning about the size of the numbers and the operation. For example, 9 + 38 must be less than 50 because 10 + 40 is 50 and both addends (9 and 38) are less than 10 and 40 respectively. From time to time, you should inject these ideas into conversations when students don't offer them.

MORE OR LESS—ADDITIONAL EXAMPLES

A. Understanding for this routine is rooted in activities and opportunities in kindergarten and early first grade. Students at these levels can reason about the results of addition and subtraction, too. You can provide students with physical or visual representations to help them make sense of the quantities being added as well as their comparisons. Example A shows what *More or Less* might look like for these students. Here, three 10 frames are posed in order to compare the sum of these frames with 10. Earlier experiences might first begin with two 10 frames. Even so, you should provide opportunties for three 10 frames at some point. In this example, students might discuss giving three to five and seeing that only two more empty spaces are left. Others might put the two threes together noting that it makes more than half of the 10 frame.

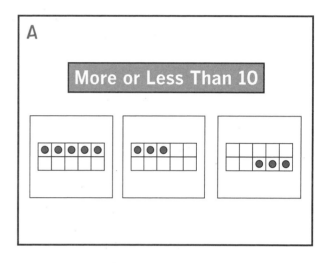

B. Proficiency with making and decomposing friendly numbers and benchmarks is another lynchpin for student success. As with example A, you can expose students to these ideas and comparisons in the earliest grades. Ten frames are one way to do so. Dominos or dot cards, as shown in example B, are other options. Now, students are presented with four cards. This is intentional in order to elicit ideas that 10 and 10 make 20 and that only one row (6 and 4) makes 10. Some students might only be able to see the cards vertically at first. Thus, your discussion afterwards will be critical for helping them see other strategies or possibilities. As with Example A, students in Example B might rely on counting all of the dots or pips. As this happens, it is critical that you highlight and reinforce more efficient strategies offered by other students. You should acknowledge students who count by ones and ask them to think about how their results compare to other grouping and counting strategies.

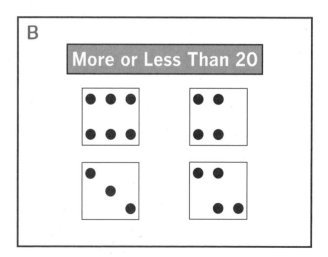

C. *More or Less* works with any operation and any size or type of number. You likely won't offer all of the expressions in Example C all at once to students in any one grade. Instead, the example is used to show what different options might look like in different grades. The first prompt, 7 × 5 is an example of how students might think about basic facts. The second prompt, 712 – 644, shows how three-digit subtraction might work or subtraction in general. Here, students have to consider if the difference will be more or less than 25. Students might try to regroup, some might count back, some might count up, and others might think about the space between 650 and 700 being greater than 25 itself.

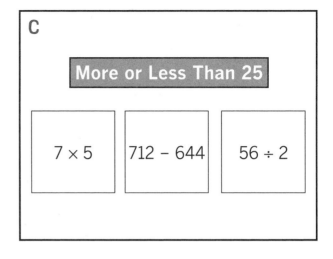

D. Similar to Example C, the expressions in Example D are provided to give a sense of the range of the routine. However, Example D is different in another way. Its *comparison number* (81) is not a friendly number or benchmark. These numbers are good to include as comparisons in the routine. Keep in mind that you might reserve them for students who have experienced the routine a bit. Numbers like 81, 276, and so on can be much harder to think about. First, working with friendly, benchmark numbers helps students build a foundation that they can then apply to these more *complicated* numbers. The strategies students use are likely to remain similar. For example, the first prompt (163 – 75) might be thought of as a combined difference of 25 (100 and 75) and 63 (100 and 163), which is more than 81. In the second, students might quickly reason that 3 × 30 = 90 so 3 × 34 must be more than 81. And in the last, students might think that 600 ÷ 6 = 100 and 592 is quite close to 600 so then the quotient must be close to 100.

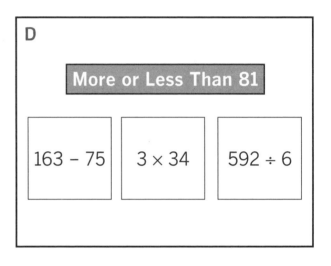

MORE OR LESS VARIATION—FRACTIONS

Student challenges with operations and sense making often increase when fractions are included in problems and computations. In these situations, reasoning about addends or estimating sums and differences is even more important. *More or Less* can be adjusted so that students can transfer their ideas and strategies to these *new* numbers.

E. Early use of *More or Less* should simply ask students to compare the results of fractions to 1. In time, you can use multiple addends so that students confront comparisons of larger whole numbers such as 5 or 6. Using this routine with fractions, also helps students revisit ideas such as relating fractions to benchmarks such as 0, $\frac{1}{2}$, and 1. This skill is helpful for comparing fractions. It is also quite helpful for estimating results of adding or subtracting fractions. In Example E, students are to consider if $\frac{4}{10} + \frac{3}{4}$ is more or less than 1. Reasoning that $\frac{4}{10}$ is almost half and that $\frac{3}{4}$ is a good bit more than $\frac{1}{2}$ enables them to conclude that the sum is more than one. This determination is most useful when exact sums are needed and they must consider if their results are reasonable. The right example is a glimpse at how subtraction with fractions might play out in the routine.

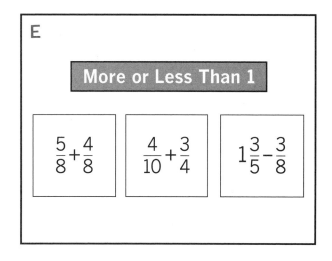

F. Example E suggests that students should first work with comparing results to 1. But in time, you can begin to pose more interesting expressions and comparisons. Yet again, the strategies are likely to be similar. Students might consider how close each addend is to 0, $\frac{1}{2}$, or 1 and possibly 2 (as in the right prompt). In the left prompt, common denominators and exact calculations might be considered. Strategies that rely on exact solutions is fine. In some cases, students can find exacts more efficiently especially if all terms have common denominators. But common denominators are not always used. When denominators aren't common, as with the left prompt, students might think about the sum of $\frac{1}{8}$ and $\frac{2}{4}$ being less than 1 and so the other addend must be at least a little more than 2, which it is not.

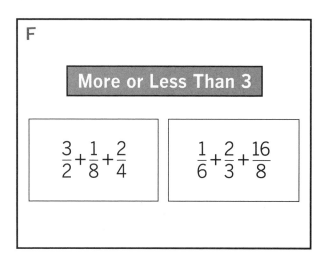

MORE OR LESS VARIATION—UNKNOWNS

Your first reaction to Examples G and H is probably "Our kids don't have to do that!" But, can they? Elementary students are expected to write equations to solve problems with unknowns in any position. Using equations in this routine provides exposure and discussion to help students develop comfort and confidence with equations. It also helps them make sense of how numbers are related to one another in an equation—which is something they have to do.

G. Each of the *More or Less* prompts in Example G could easily represent an elementary word problem. As we know, student success with word problems can be disappointing. Often, we wonder if our students even considered if their answer made sense. Sometimes that consideration is in relation to the context of the problem or the question that it is asking. Other times, it is in relation to the results of their computations. What if you strip away everything but the equation and ask them to simply think about the numbers in the problem? The result is Example G. Here, it's likely that many elementary students will quickly recognize that the value of the unknown in the first prompt must be much more than 25. In fact, the others are quite obvious, too. For example, if they know that there are four 25s in 100, the unknown in the middle equation must be more than 25.

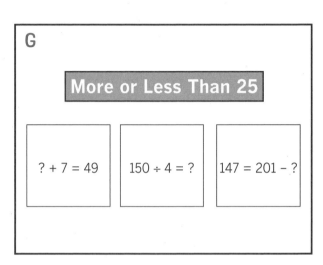

G

More or Less Than 25

? + 7 = 49	150 ÷ 4 = ?	147 = 201 − ?

NOTES

_____

_____

_____

_____

_____

_____

_____

_____

_____

_____

_____

H. You can apply fractions and unknowns in equations to *More or Less*. You can easily adjust it to use with decimals and even unknowns in equations that have decimal numbers. Example H shows how decimals might be incorporated into the routine. This adaptation of the routine is better for students in middle to late fifth grade or students who need enrichment and/or extension opportunities. As with other unknowns, students do not have to apply procedure to solving the equations. Substitution and reasoning will suffice. The first equation is one that students often get wrong when applying procedure rather than reasoning. This happens as the numbers stoke a basic fact memory ($9 + 8 = 17$). But when you ask them to think about the unknown being more or less than 8, they are forced to pause and consider how adding $\frac{7}{10}$ to a whole number affects the sum (it will have $\frac{7}{10}$). In the last example, students who recognize that $8 \div 1 = 8$ will conclude that $8.4 \div 0.4$ must be greater because 0.4 is smaller than 1 meaning more will fit in 1, 8, or ultimately 8.4. The numbers used in this equation might provoke students to find an exact quotient (2.1). The debate will be which is more efficient and does efficiency change based on the numbers in the equation.

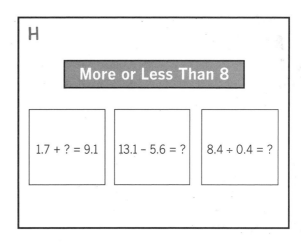

H

More or Less Than 8

| $1.7 + ? = 9.1$ | $13.1 - 5.6 = ?$ | $8.4 \div 0.4 = ?$ |

NOTES

_____

_____

_____

_____

_____

_____

_____

_____

_____

_____

THIS OR THAT? (ESTIMATING AND COMPARING)

About the Routine

There are few, if any of us, who haven't played the game *Would You Rather?* Often, we play it with outlandish choices causing us to consider which is truly the better choice. Players quickly defend their thinking with reasoning that is sometimes rational and sometimes not. There are mathematical versions that ask students to pick one group of base-10 blocks over another or to tell which basic fact is greater than another. Often, the choices in these versions are rather mundane and the reasoning in these versions is not much more than recall. *This or That?* is a take on *Would You Rather?* in which students have to determine if they would want one thing over another. The twist is that the comparisons are grounded in reasoning about number and operation. In some cases, students will estimate. In other comparisons, students will reason about properties and relationships between expressions. Of course, there will be students who use exacts to make their comparisons. In some cases, the exacts are entirely appropriate. But in others,

Treasure of Gold Coins

THIS	THAT
39×48	2,000
410×8	2,000
$12 \times 20 \times 10$	2,000

exact calculations are simply inefficient for making a choice. In the featured example, students are asked to determine if they would want this treasure of gold coins or that. In each proposition, students compare an expression to a benchmark of 2,000. As with other routines, students determine a choice, share their reasoning with a partner, and discuss different strategies with the entire group.

Why It Matters

This routine helps students:

- estimate values and solutions to expressions (MP2);

- consider efficient methods for finding results (MP2 and MP6);

- consider alternative strategies for computation and comparison (MP2);

- reason about the strategies that they are using (MP3);

- communicate their reasoning to others (MP3);

All tasks can be downloaded for your use at **resources.corwin.com/ jumpstartroutines/elementary**

- develop confidence in their reasoning and computations;
- enhance their ability to determine reasonableness of answers or solutions (MP2);
- develop flexibility, efficiency, and accuracy (computational fluency) (MP6);
- compare their ideas to the reasoning of others (MP3); and
- look for and make use of number relationships and patterns within operations (MP7 and MP8).

What They Should Understand First

This or That? builds on number concepts, operations, and properties that students understand to some extent. In the featured example, your students should have understanding of multiplication of multi-digit numbers. They should have worked with multiplying multiples of 10 before this version. They should be comfortable with different estimation strategies including rounding and using compatibles. You can reinforce these strategies through instruction and other routines such as *About or Between*

(Routine 15, page 116). In some situations, such as the third expression in this example, understanding of properties of operations is needed. Students should be able to think about numbers flexibly. They do not have to master the basic facts or procedures for computations to engage in this routine. In fact, for many students this routine will increase their accuracy and consistency with these procedures or at the least help them consider if their calculations are reasonable.

What to Do

1. Select two or three sets of expressions to compare. Compare each to anticipate what students might do.

2. Direct students to compare each row of expressions deciding if they would prefer *This or That?* (determine which expression is greater). Consider posing one comparison at a time.

3. Remind students that this is a mental mathematics activity and that exact answers aren't required though they can use exact figures if they are able to find them.

4. Provide time for students to reason and compare.

5. Direct students to share their findings and reasoning with a partner.

6. Facilitate a discussion about how students compared the expressions to make their decisions about *This or That?* Some questions to ask include:

   » How did you know the expression was greater than the other?

   » Did you find an exact amount or did you find an estimated amount or *about*?

   » Why was it better to use friendly numbers in this comparison?

   » Did you notice a pattern or think about a property of multiplication or division?

   » Does this pattern always work? When might it not work?

   » Can you think of another expression that would be greater than _____ or less than _____?

   » Did anyone compare the expressions differently?

   » How could thinking about expressions in this way help you determine if your exact answer is reasonable?

7. Optional: Record student strategies on board, white board, or document camera. Doing this can help other students *see* classmates' reasoning.

8. Optional: Find exact solutions after discussion about estimates and reasoning.

9. Honor and explore both accurate and flawed reasoning.

Anticipated Strategies for This Example

Treasure of Gold Coins

THIS	THAT
39 × 48	2,000
410 × 8	2,000
12 × 20 × 10	2,000

The featured example for *This or That?* has students compare an expression to a benchmark number. Quite a few students will be tempted to find exact results of the expressions before comparing them to 2,000. Other students will estimate or reason about the results. In the first expression, they might consider that 40 × 50 is 2,000. 39 is less than 40 and 48 is less than 50 so *this* is less than *that*. Students might be overwhelmed to think about a three-digit factor in the second expression. But again, thinking of the expression in a more-friendly way can help them determine a choice. 400 × 8 is 3,200 so *this* is the better choice. Some students might suggest that a three-digit number times another number will have to be more than 2,000. In this case, they are correct. To counter the thinking, you can provide a prompt the following day such as 135 × 4 so they can determine if their generalization is always true. The same may be true for the third expression. Some students will believe that the product of three factors will always be a very large number. In this case, 12 × 20 × 10 is greater than 2,000. But, would it be if one of the factors was approximately half?

THIS OR THAT?—ADDITIONAL EXAMPLES

A. Students in any grade can consider *This or That?* Example A offers prompts for the routine if used early in first grade. The different ideas captured in each row are intended to show the range of the routine. You might choose not to mix the ideas of addition, subtraction, and comparison in the same routine until later in the year. Student understanding and misconception will appear here and with other examples. Students might determine 4 + 1 to be greater than 7 because they are adding or because there are two numbers in their choice. You can use student reasoning to create new prompts and to advance their understanding. For example, students might believe that subtraction always yields a smaller number. So, they would determine that 4 is more than 12 − 10. A day or so later, you might have them compare 12 − 2 and 9 or 18 − 6 and 4. The last row is a simple suggestion for comparing numbers. It might occur early in first grade and be revisited throughout the year with ever changing numbers and place value arrangements.

A

Treasure of Gold Coins

THIS	THAT
4 + 1	7
12 − 10	4
3 tens	1 ten 9 ones

B. Example B changes the desirable from gold coins to ice cream sandwiches. Mathematically, it has a more significant adjustment. Here, students shift from comparing expressions and single values to comparing two expressions. It also shows how you can incorporate basic facts into the routine. Other ideas about basic understanding of multiplication appear in the second row. Students should determine that 9×4 is greater than 6×4 because it is more groups of four. The routine can also uncover useful patterns. For example, in the third row students can determine that 6×9 is greater than 5×8 simply because both factors are greater than the others.

C. *This or That?* allows for students to find and make use of patterns and properties like that described in Example B. Example C not only shows how the routine might play out with three-digit addends it also helps students examine patterns within addition and subtraction of these numbers. The last comparison is an example. In it, students might be tempted to add all of the numbers which is viable. But if you look carefully, you see that two of the addends are the same in both expressions therefore *that* is greater because 25 is greater than 23. Nothing else needs considering. The example also plays on other misconceptions that students might have. For example, some think that subtraction will always yield a result less than addition. However, the difference of $800 - 209$ is a little less than 600 whereas the sum of $314 + 318$ is a little more than 600 so *that* is the better choice.

B

Ice Cream Sandwiches

THIS	THAT
3×6	20
4×6	9×4
5×8	6×9

C

Ice Cream Sandwiches

THIS	THAT
$800 - 209$	$314 + 318$
$700 - 619$	$35 + 47 + 50$
$17 + 23 + 30$	$17 + 30 + 25$

D. Changing the topic of the routine keeps it fresh. Gold and ice cream are desirable but possibly not as desirable as more recess. Again, the comparables are designed to foster thinking, estimation, and application of computation strategies. Comparing $700 \div 76$ and $523 \div 25$ can be daunting for a fifth grader. But, your discussion has the potential to uncover that the comparison can be done by thinking about how many groups of 70 are in 700 versus how many groups of 25 are in 250 and then ultimately 500. It is also easy to see how discussion, about these strategies, has the potential to increase precision with calculations. As with other examples, Example D shows how the routine can play on potential student misconceptions yet again. Students might be tempted to think that $814 \div 31$ will be larger than $64 \div 2$ because the dividend and divisor are larger. The third expression gives you an idea how operations could be mingled during the routine.

D

Hours of Recess

THIS	THAT
$700 \div 76$	$523 \div 25$
$814 \div 31$	$64 \div 2$
$517 \div 50$	8×41

NOTES

THIS OR THAT? VARIATION—COUNTING

You can leverage *This or That?* to introduce or reinforce basic principles of counting and comparison. You can do this with images and objects. You might use *real* things such as gummy bears. But ordinary, classroom things might be used to represent ideas as well. For example, you might use two-sided counters to represent gold coins.

E. How would kindergarteners compare the gummy bears in Example E of *This or That?* Some may simply see that there are more on the right. The images can then be used to reinforce the meaning of the related digits or counts. Counting is one way that students might compare as well. Discussions about how students count to compare have potential to be quite rich. Students might talk about how many were counted in all. Others might talk about counting the *extras* while ignoring what was the same in both pictures (top and bottom rows of 6).

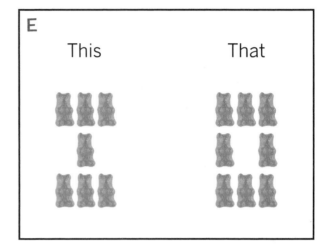

F. Counting larger amounts is a reasonable application of the routine. Comparing exacts and estimates is another option. Example F has students compare two pictures in which one amount of brownies can be found with certainty while the other must be estimated. Students will always bring novel reasoning to problems and mathematics. Some may choose the brownies on the left because they don't like nuts in their brownies as seen on the right. You should acknowledge their reasoning and then redirect them to size and quantity.

Example E image source: vikif/iStock.com; Example F image sources: ArxOnt/iStock.com, blackwaterimages/iStock.com

THIS OR THAT? VARIATION—FRACTIONS AND DECIMALS

Computing fractions and decimals holds the potential for wildly inaccurate results. Students who are able to consider the reasonableness of sums and differences are more likely to determine when their computed results are impossible. *This or That?* is a chance to develop estimation and reasoning strategies that work with fractions and decimals.

G. Estimating sums and differences of fractions and mixed numbers with unlike denominators is perfect for this routine. In Example G, students once again consider which amount of recess would be most desirable. However, they now must think about fractions of time. In the first, students might choose *this* because it is addition. Some might choose *that* because the whole number is greater. And, some may reason that $8+\frac{1}{2}$ is $8\frac{1}{2}$ whereas $9-\frac{5}{8}$ is a little less than $8\frac{1}{2}$ because $\frac{5}{8}$ is a little more than $\frac{1}{2}$. In the second row, two fractions that are quite close to 1 will have a sum close to 2 while the difference of *that* is exactly $1\frac{1}{3}$, which is not close to 2. In the last comparison, *this* is more than 5 while *that* is less than 5.

G

Hours of Recess

THIS	THAT
$8 + \frac{1}{2}$	$9 - \frac{5}{8}$
$\frac{7}{8} + \frac{8}{9}$	$2 - \frac{2}{3}$
$3\frac{1}{3} + 1\frac{7}{8}$	$2\frac{1}{4} + 1\frac{1}{2} + \frac{9}{10}$

H. Any student or parent with limited cell phone data knows how quickly it vanishes. Having more data is simply better than having less. In Example H, students are presented with gigabytes of data as contexts for quantity. As with whole numbers in early grades, students can be simply challenged to consider the meaning of place value as in the first comparison in this example. In time, you can prompt your students to compare sums and differences. Prompts can be clever as with the second comparison in this example. Here, the same digits are presented in the same order. Many students will contend that the two are equal. Some will note that 71 is much greater than 14 and thus computation is unnecessary. Yet, some students will need to compute to prove this contention to be true. The third comparison shows again how you can mix the operations and how you can use multi-digit decimals.

H

Gigabytes of Data

THIS	THAT
0.26	0.62
14 + 7.1	1.4 + 71
13.54 − 12.5	6.88 + 2.98

FINDING ONE AND ALL (EFFICIENT COMPUTATION)

About the Routine

Patterns help students solve problems, recall basic facts, and make sense of concepts. Human brains are wired to look for and take note of patterns. However, it can be hard to find someone else's pattern. In other words, it can be hard for students to identify patterns that their teachers already know about. Students may see all sorts of patterns in a chart or string of numbers but it might not be the *desired* pattern, relationship, or idea. Unsuccessful recognition of intended patterns can lead to stalled discussions, closed or rapid-fire questions, and ultimately frustration for both the teacher and the student. One way around this challenge is to ask students to share all of the patterns they notice in a given situation. Another way is to arrange expressions, equations, and other recordings in intentional ways so that patterns become obvious to students. Number strings are an example of intentional arrangements that help students see patterns in expressions and equations. Today, number strings are rather common. But for many teachers, these strings were not features of their learning and become challenging to create and thus easy to avoid. *Finding One and All* is a routine that presents two related number strings for students to complete and discuss. The two related number strings are

Use one to find them all.	
8 × 6 = 48	8 × 5 =
8 × 60 =	8 × 50 =
8 × 61 =	8 × 51 =
8 × 600 =	8 × 500 =
8 × 601 =	8 × 501 =

presented at the same time. Students are given one expression and then given time to use the known to find other solutions. The class shares solutions and discusses how one expression was used to solve both strings of numbers. Patterns and relationships are discussed. This routine isolates related expressions so that students can focus on the patterns and relationships. As with other routines, it is designed as a mental math activity. Students might have charts and calculators during the discussion to confirm that calculations are accurate.

 All tasks can be downloaded for your use at **resources.corwin.com/ jumpstartroutines/elementary**

Why It Matters

This routine helps students:

- reason about relationships between operations and quantities (MP2);
- identify patterns in mathematics (MP7);
- make generalizations about mathematical ideas to create shortcuts (MP8);
- reinforce understanding of mathematical concepts;
- develop computational and problem-solving strategies grounded in patterns (MP1); and
- communicate their reasoning to others (MP3).

What They Should Understand First

The featured example of *Finding One and All* is perfect to use some time in the middle of fourth grade through fifth and even sixth grade. Students should have firm understanding of multiplication. They should show that they have different strategies for finding products. They should be able to manipulate multiplication situations in which one, two, or more groups are added or taken away. Students should have worked with multi-digit multiplication and be able to use the distributive property to some extent.

Though students can always represent expressions with arrays and area models, they should be capable of manipulating expressions without those representations. Students should be able to make sense of products of factors that are multiples of tens or hundreds as well. As with other routines, basic fact mastery isn't required as a basic fact can be provided as the one known in the string or strings. Work with the routine intends to strengthen student recall of facts.

What to Do

1. Identify patterns or strategies that need to be practiced.

2. Create two number strings. See Example C for advice on how to do so efficiently.

3. Present both number strings to students with one known provided. It is optional to present one set of strings at a time. The second string may be reserved for the following day due to discussion length and other time considerations.

4. Have students find the solutions to the other expressions presented in the first column.

5. Have students discuss with a partner how they found their solutions before bringing the group back together.

6. Discuss with the class how solutions were found. During discussion, questions to highlight include:
   - » How did you find the solution to (insert expression)?
   - » How was that expression related to the one above it?
   - » Which expression was easiest for you to realize?
   - » Which expression was most difficult?
   - » How can you explain the shortcut you took of adding zeroes?
   - » What surprised you about the pattern?
   - » Have you used this relationship before?
   - » What is a new expression you could solve because of the pattern in this number string?
   - » How are the two strings related? (after the second column is discussed)

7. Consider adding a new expression and asking if the expression fits with the patterns and relationships examined during the routine.

8. Celebrate student success, communication, and effort.

9. Challenge students to be on the lookout for computations during the mathematics class that could be solved with the patterns and/or relationships discussed during the routine.

Anticipated Strategies for This Example

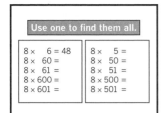

Use one to find them all.	
8 × 6 = 48	8 × 5 =
8 × 60 =	8 × 50 =
8 × 61 =	8 × 51 =
8 × 600 =	8 × 500 =
8 × 601 =	8 × 501 =

Student accuracy during this routine is likely to fluctuate. Providing students with fact charts may be helpful for some versions of the routine such as this featured example. Students who recall facts well might be challenged to extend or transfer their recall abilities to more complex expressions. Students may apply observational shortcuts such as *adding* or *counting zeroes* without being able to describe why zeroes can be *added*. In the first string, students should be able to use the known to find and explain that 8 × 60 is similar to 8 × six tens and then some will transfer that to 8 × 600 thinking of it as 8 × six hundreds. Some students may choose to solve expressions by looking for relationships rather than going in order. For example, they might find 8 × 60 and then more to 8 × 600 rather than move from 8 × 60 to 8 × 61 and so on. In the second column, students might use patterns from the left string to find results for the string on the right. At the least, they may use the known 8 × 6 = 48 to derive the first expression of 8 × 5. However, some students might proceed through the string on the right without noticing the relationship between the two strings.

FINDING ONE AND ALL—ADDITIONAL EXAMPLES

A. Students in all grade levels should work with patterns in computations. This helps reinforce basic computations and make connections between them. Doing this routinely enables students to see that ideas in math are related rather than isolated. It develops efficiency and flexibility leading to fluency. *Using 10* is a basic fact strategy that students use to add nine or eight and sometimes seven. But many students, even those that can recall those facts quickly, don't see how adding nine is related to adding 19 or adding 29. They don't recognize that using 10 or making 10 is applicable to a whole slew of other addends. In Example A, students are afforded that opportunity. They can see that 9 + 6 is the same as 19 + 6 in that they make the next 10 and have some more leftover. Keep in mind that some students might see the pattern differently and simply change the number of tens. This is fine and worth discussion with the group as to why it works and how it can be thought of as a shortcut.

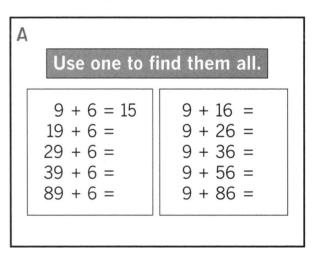

A

Use one to find them all.	
9 + 6 = 15	9 + 16 =
19 + 6 =	9 + 26 =
29 + 6 =	9 + 36 =
39 + 6 =	9 + 56 =
89 + 6 =	9 + 86 =

B. Patterns in addition are often easier for students to recognize than patterns within subtraction. This might be attributed to better comfort or proficiency with addition. Regardless of the reason, students need ample opportunities to look for patterns within subtraction as well as addition. They can extend basic fact strategies as described in Example A. They can also grapple with new and different patterns. Example B reveals two of those useful patterns. In the first string, the same amount is taken away from an amount that continues to increase by one. Because of this, the difference increases by the same amount. A different, yet related, pattern appears in the string on the right. Here, one more is taken away from the same amount each time. Because one more is taken away, the difference decreases by one in each subsequent equation. These are just two of the many patterns waiting to be *discovered* in the routine.

B

Use one to find them all.

$14 - 7 = 7$	$14 - 7 =$
$15 - 7 =$	$14 - 8 =$
$16 - 7 =$	$14 - 9 =$
$17 - 7 =$	$14 - 10 =$
$18 - 7 =$	$14 - 11 =$
$19 - 7 =$	$14 - 12 =$

C. Example C is somewhat similar to the featured example of *Finding One and All*. It serves as a way to illustrate how these number strings might be created. As noted previously, good strings can be hard for teachers to write. One way to overcome this is to write an expression and think about the patterns, relationships, or properties to highlight. For Example C, a teacher jotted down 68×12. Then, she thought about how it might be solved by identifying partials and the relationship to 70. She then wrote down the different partials including 6×2, 8×2, 60×2, and so on. She reviewed the expressions and put them into an order that seemed to make sense. Though some order is necessary, the exact order of expressions is debatable. She then used a similar process for the second string in which she recorded 7×10, 7×2, 7×12, and the other expressions. She rearranged the order then presented as is. Creating examples of the routine might be first done well with a colleague to discuss what makes sense. Working together also has the potential to provide twice as many examples to use with students.

C

Use one to find them all.

$6 \times 2 = 12$	$7 \times 10 =$
$60 \times 2 =$	$70 \times 10 =$
$8 \times 2 =$	$70 \times 2 =$
$68 \times 2 =$	$70 \times 12 =$
$68 \times 10 =$	$2 \times 12 =$
$68 \times 12 =$	$68 \times 12 =$

D. Like subtraction, division presents challenges to thinking about patterns and relationships. However, you can use this routine to not only expose students to the patterns, but to deepen their understanding and increase their number of strategies to approach division problems. A chief strategy for dividing with multi-digit numbers is to decompose the dividend and find partial quotients. Example D shows how this might play out in the routine. The strings were written in a process described in Example C. Here, 78 ÷ 6 and 91 ÷ 7 were the initial expressions to solve. Ideas about how the dividends might be decomposed were thought about and recorded. The strings were then arranged from those ideas. The additional expressions in those strings, 780 ÷ 6 and 910 ÷ 7, were then added to extend the strings. 780 ÷ 60 or 910 ÷ 70 could have just have easily been added.

D

Use one to find them all.

$6 \div 6 = 1$	$7 \div 7 =$
$12 \div 6 =$	$14 \div 7 =$
$18 \div 6 =$	$21 \div 7 =$
$60 \div 6 =$	$70 \div 7 =$
$78 \div 6 =$	$91 \div 7 =$
$780 \div 6 =$	$910 \div 7 =$

NOTES

FINDING ONE AND ALL VARIATION—MAKE 10

Making 10 or combinations of 10 is one of the most important ideas that young mathematicians learn about. For many, they are able to recall the combinations rather quickly. Yet, successful students are often limited in how they apply and extend these combinations to other situations. Examples E and F show how combinations of 10 might be leveraged for first and second graders. These examples could be easily modified to examine decimal applications of combinations in later grades as 0.6 + 0.4 is quite similar to 6 + 4.

E. How will first graders find 16 + 4 when they know that 6 + 4 = 10? Will they start with 16 and count on 4? Will they recognize that 16 is 10 more than 6 and conclude that the sum must be 10 more than 10? Will they almost instantly see how a 10 is made and determine that 14 and 6 makes a new 10? These questions most certainly will be answered through Example E. The other expressions should then confirm that students do or do not see these relationships. Note that the expressions skip tens intentionally to get a better sense of how students are using the relationships between expressions as it is possible that students might simply change the sums without thinking about the changing addends. The expression on the right is likely better suited for second or third graders. It is provided to illustrate different examples of using 10 only.

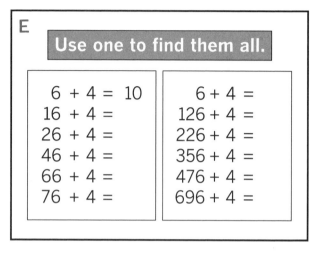

E

Use one to find them all.

6 + 4 = 10	6 + 4 =
16 + 4 =	126 + 4 =
26 + 4 =	226 + 4 =
46 + 4 =	356 + 4 =
66 + 4 =	476 + 4 =
76 + 4 =	696 + 4 =

F. Example F builds on making 10 in another way. Here, students make 10 but have an additional 10 to work with. It might be used a day after Example E is used with students. Discussion about this string should focus on how both addends have a number of tens and that another 10 is made from the ones in each addend. Again, the pattern in the first addend is not sequential (skips 36 and 56) intentionally.

F

Use one to find them all.

6 + 4 = 10	6 + 4 =
16 + 14 =	126 + 14 =
26 + 14 =	226 + 14 =
46 + 14 =	356 + 14 =
66 + 14 =	476 + 14 =
76 + 14 =	696 + 14 =

FINDING ONE AND ALL VARIATION—USING 10

Knowing combinations of 10 is critical because it can be applied to all sorts of other computations. Knowing 10 easily extends to using 10. When students use 10, they make a 10 and have some leftover. This too is a basic fact strategy that many students recognize and use but don't always extend to two- or three-digit addends.

G. Example G begins with the use 10 fact 8 + 4. The pattern in the left string builds on it. The example here also shows how the routine can be modified to reinforce and/or serve any purpose. Instead of the right string beginning with 8 + 4 it instead begins with 18 + 7 that was solved in the left string. This new string gives students the opportunity to transfer using 10 to different two-digit addends or to make use of the pattern that a sum increases by 10 as an addend is increased by 10. For example, the sum of 38 + 7 is 10 more than 28 + 7 because 38 is 10 more than 28.

G

Use one to find them all.

$8 + 2 = 10$	$18 + 7 =$
$8 + 4 =$	$28 + 7 =$
$8 + 6 =$	$38 + 7 =$
$8 + 7 =$	$58 + 7 =$
$18 + 7 =$	$88 + 7 =$
$48 + 7 =$	$98 + 7 =$

H. Example H is an example of how using 10 can be applied to subtraction. Some students might count back through the 10 while others might count up to find the difference. This example also illustrates two different patterns that might be explored on the same day or on different days. On the left side, the string has students apply a use 10 strategy for subtraction to related minuends. It also has them consider how a difference increases by 10 as a minuend is increased by 10. On the right side, students can again leverage a using 10 fact but are instead funneled to the relationship that occurs when 10 more is taken from a number each successive time.

H

Use one to find them all.

$13 - 9 = 4$	$73 - 9 =$
$23 - 9 =$	$73 - 19 =$
$33 - 9 =$	$73 - 29 =$
$43 - 9 =$	$73 - 39 =$
$73 - 9 =$	$73 - 49 =$
$173 - 9 =$	$173 - 49 =$

ANOTHER WAY TO SAY IT (EFFICIENT COMPUTATION)

About the Routine

To be fluent means to be flexible, efficient, and accurate (National Research Council, 2001). Knowing a collection of strategies and applying each of them to every computation is not quite the intent. So, the definition of fluency might also include *appropriate*. Appropriate means that students can determine a fitting strategy for a given calculation or computation (Arizona Department of Education, 2018). It means that students consider if decomposing makes sense when confronting two, four-digit addends such as 3,477 + 4,999. It might even include consideration of which approach—mental mathematics, paper/pencil, or calculator—is most appropriate for the numbers in the problem. But before a student can be efficient or appropriate, they must have opportunities to *rethink* an expression rather than simply calculate it. Students need to listen to how others might approach a problem so that they can think about how they might deal with it differently. In this routine, students are prompted with two or three expressions. *They are not asked to solve the expressions.* Instead, they are asked to say and think about ways they might adjust, reorder, or decompose the numbers in

What is another way to say it?
39 + 28
47 + 25
58 + 44

the problem. Students then have an opportunity to hear about others' ideas for working with the same numbers. Discussion should then transition to debate about which strategies are possibly more useful, more efficient, or more appropriate. The featured example presents three expressions with two-digit addends. But, the routine can be modified in a wide variety of ways so that operations and numbers align to student proficiencies.

online resources
All tasks can be downloaded for your use at **resources.corwin.com/ jumpstartroutines/elementary**

Why It Matters

This routine helps students:

- consider how expressions might be adjusted, reordered, or decomposed (MP2);
- apply properties of operations for developing efficiencies (MP7);
- develop strategies to become computationally fluent (MP6);
- make use of efficient strategies so that decisions to use tools for calculations can be done so strategically (MP5);
- build confidence with computation and computational strategies;
- look for and manipulate patterns and structure within relationships (MP8);
- reinforce ideas about friendly numbers or benchmarks;
- practice computation to improve precision (MP2); and
- strengthen or acquire computational strategies by exchanging ideas with others (MP3).

What They Should Understand First

Some students perceive mathematics as the pursuit of answers. They might use strategies, but their focus is on the result. This routine intends for students to think about how they *could* compute rather than actually computing. To be successful, students must have learned about strategies for working with the designated operations. In this featured example, it would be reasonable to expect students to understand place value, the meaning of addition, how place values are added, and how tools can be used to demonstrate their understanding. Students do not necessarily need to be flawless in application or execution of these strategies. The routine can support that development. Also note that it is highly likely that the routine will need to be modeled the first time it is used so that students understand the goal to be restating the expression rather than finding the solution. It is important to note that students should be able to think flexibly about numbers and be able to decompose the same number in many ways. Routines like *Show It 3* (Routine 6, page 55), *How Can You Make It?* (Routine 7, page 62), and *The Mighty Ten* (Routine 8, page 69) can help them practice these concepts.

What to Do

1. Create three or four expressions for students to examine.

2. Have students consider the operation and how they might adjust the expression. The routine is intended to be a mental activity. Some might need the support of a personal dry erase board to record their thinking. Look for students with these tools to be reworking the expression instead of evaluating it. The intent is not to find the solution but to consider how the expression could be manipulated.

3. Have students share their strategy with a partner. Listen for a strategy that would be a good place to begin the whole group discussion. Consider how student strategies might be recorded.

4. Bring the class back together to discuss strategies for finding solutions efficiently. Be mindful that some examples may not be efficient or strategies at all. Questions to ask for the featured example might include:

   » How did you think about the addends?

   » Why did you decide to make a 10?

   » Did anyone think about the problem differently?

   » How is your strategy different than another student's?

   » Why was it more efficient for you to think about the problem in that way?

   » Which strategy makes the most sense to you?

» What is another problem that you could write to use this strategy with? (Note: This would extend the expression and may mean that others aren't considered during the routine.)

5. Consider adding a new strategy to advance student thinking if needed/appropriate.

6. Celebrate student effort and engagement in the discussion.

Anticipated Strategies for This Example

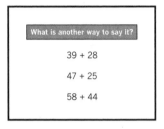

Each expression has the potential to be solved in a variety of ways though these were written intentionally to see if students adjust to make tens. Your discussion with students should focus on efficiency and appropriateness. In the featured example, students might decompose 39 + 28 into 30 + 20 + 9 + 8 or something similar. Some might decompose just one addend. Those students might start with 39 and count on by tens and ones. Some students might need to count on by ones starting with 39. Some students might adjust the addends giving one from 28 to make 40 + 27. All strategies in this example are acceptable. Regardless of where students are with their strategies, they can be exposed to other ideas and asked to think about how their strategy relates in terms of accuracy and efficiency. Students who are counting on by ones will benefit from thinking about counting on by tens and ones. In turn, students who use partial sums will benefit from thinking about adjusting. Adjusters will recognize that other strategies are viable and possibly more appropriate as the addends change.

ANOTHER WAY TO SAY IT—ADDITIONAL EXAMPLES

A. Fluency with two- and three-digit addends is grounded in learning basic facts through strategies and relationships. You can easily modify this routine to feature basic facts and to help students think about how these seemingly *simple* calculations might be adjusted. Keep in mind that basic fact recall is about automatic recall. However, this occurs through a large quantity of exposure and practice. Until achieved, students need strategies for recalling facts. Example A offers two columns of expressions. You can adjust the number of expressions to best suit student need and time allocation. Also note that the facts in the left column are make- or use-10 facts while those on the right are use-doubles facts. Mingling of fact strategies might not be the best place to begin this work. They are offered together in this example to give a sense of what you might do with base facts. You can easily edit the downloadable slides so that one column is removed or changed to coincide with the other.

A

What is another way to say it?	
9 + 7	5 + 4
5 + 9	3 + 8
6 + 8	7 + 8

B. This routine works well to develop fluency with upper elementary students. Example B shows how you might use three-digit numbers to appropriately challenge them. Of course, four-digit addends and subtraction would also work well. After students share strategies, shift the discussion to consider how efficient or appropriate the different strategies are. This discussion becomes quite valuable as students in these grades begin to learn about standard algorithms. It helps them determine when the algorithm is helpful and when it is a hinderance. As with two-digit addends, students are likely to use similar strategies like decomposing to add partials or adjusting to add compatible numbers.

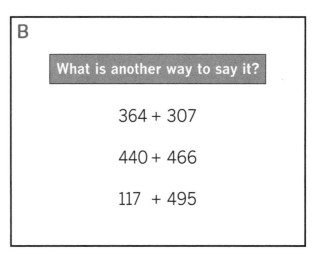

C. Thinking about addition strategies, or even addition in general, is less challenging for many students and adults. You can leverage a well-developed understanding of addition and addition strategies to help students build similar understanding with subtraction. Nevertheless, students must practice and discuss subtraction in routines including this one, and so Example C shows what that might look like. Strategies will be unique and diverse just as it is with addition. Students might adjust in the first example by adding four to each number creating a simpler problem of 68 – 30. Others might decompose one or both numbers using partial differences to arrive at the difference. Students will adjust and decompose larger numbers as well though there are more ways to apply either of these strategies. Because of this, you may want to shift discussion to the most efficient and appropriate adjustments or decompositions. Also note that you can adjust the number of expressions or explorations as needed and that work with subtraction expressions may take longer than early work with addition.

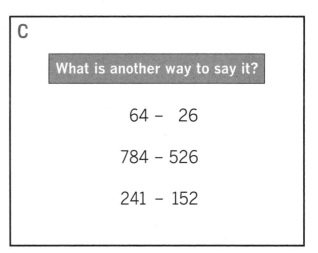

D. Identifying and using patterns in mathematics contributes to our students' success. Recognizing patterns enables generalities that allow for shortcuts and efficiencies. Working with related expressions can help students look for and use patterns when computing while strengthening ideas about how friendlier computations are related to original computations. You can help them examine, explore, and discuss patterns with this routine. Example D presents students with two expressions. The second has been changed by adding 100 to both numbers. The second can be solved quickly once that relationship is noted. However, students might not notice the change at first. It can be challenging to avoid pointing this out immediately. Instead, allow this *discovery* to appear through student observation. You can call attention to the relationship between the expressions if the students haven't already described it. The lower right expression is adjusted by 410. In your early work with this version of the routine, you might limit adjustments to easily observable changes. Changes are easier to observe when one place value, likely the ones place, does not change.

D

What is another way to say it?	
176 – 49	443 – 280
276 – 149	853 – 690

NOTES

_____

_____

_____

_____

_____

_____

_____

_____

_____

_____

_____

_____

_____

ANOTHER WAY TO SAY IT VARIATION— MULTIPLICATION AND DIVISION

Mental computation of multiplication and division is a worthwhile pursuit. These operations can be more challenging but student capacity grows as the number of opportunities to engage and discuss grows. As with addition and subtraction, students are likely to latch on to the strategy they are most comfortable and competent with regardless of the qualities of the factors or dividends and divisors posed.

E. Finding partial products, adjusting (such as double and half), and using related expressions are predominant multiplication strategies. Discussion about efficient and appropriate strategies might focus on how the expression is decomposed more so than which strategy is better, simply because some strategies such as double and half or related expressions aren't applicable. In the first expression, students might think about 9×24 as a it relates to 10×24. Others might think about it as 9×20 and 9×4. Though possible, doubling 9 and halving 24 to create 18×12 is likely impractical. You can repeat the process until students reach 72×3, but efficiency and appropriateness become obvious compromises.

E

What is another way to say it?

$$9 \times 24$$

$$6 \times 53$$

$$49 \times 7$$

F. Example F offers a view of how you might pose division expressions in this routine. There are limited strategies for division as well. But again, discussion can revolve around how students might decompose numbers and which partial quotients are easiest to find.

F

What is another way to say it?

$$92 \div 4$$

$$168 \div 4$$

$$2{,}130 \div 5$$

ANOTHER WAY TO SAY IT VARIATION— EXPLICIT CONNECTION

Students may need to *see* different strategies in order to acquire them. That is why teacher recordings are so important during this routine. However, you could also adjust the routine to prompt students to identify another way to think about an expression with possible expressions to choose from.

G. Multiplication and division may be more challenging for students to think about flexibly. The ideas presented in Example G might be a better starting point. All three expressions are the same as 50×36. Presenting three possibilities helps students expand their thinking as well as consider the pros and cons of specific strategies. You can complement this version of the routine with a closing question asking students if they have a different, more efficient way to think about the expression. Note that these examples are not intended to focus on order of operations but the mental processes of computing the given expression.

G

| What is another way to say 50×36? |

$$50 \times 30 + 50 \times 6$$

$$100 \times 36 \div 2$$

$$100 \times 18$$

H. Difficulty inherent in the operations is relative to student experience and perception. Presenting students with other ways to think about a multiplication or division expression as shared in Example G makes sense. It can be easily transferred to addition and subtraction for use in earlier grades. Again, all three are related to the expression yet the middle expression might be a bit unfriendly to think about. The last expression offers a unique idea about how it can be thought of. This expression captures the *counting up* that can be used to find the difference. This last offering could become a routine in itself.

H

| What is another way to say $90 - 26$? |

$$100 - 36$$

$$89 - 25$$

$$4 + 60$$

THE TRUTH (MEANING OF THE EQUAL SIGN)

About the Routine

Understanding the meaning of the equal sign is important in every grade and every mathematics course. Throughout mathematics, students use the meaning of the equal sign to create equations in order to solve problems and model real-world situations. Yet, many elementary students perceive the equal sign to mean *the answer*. They see it as the signpost for the *result* of computation. Unfortunately, this can be a deeply held belief that students retain well into upper elementary school and middle school. The meaning of the equal sign is taught in primary grades. Students should come to recognize that the sum or difference can be on either side of the equal sign. This necessitates that students understand that the two sides are equal. These same students may be challenged when an operation is on both sides of the equation. The problem becomes more pronounced when two different operations or multiple addends are on both sides. With continued practice, students become successful with these situations. Yet, as operations change to multiplication and division, and as numbers become more complex

TRUE or FALSE	
A. $10 + 6 = 16$	B. $16 = 8 + 7$
C. $9 + 7 = 16$	D. $16 = 11 + 5$

(number of digits or fractions), students might revert to more rudimentary *understanding* of equations and the equal sign. Their foundations for equations that appear later in middle school are unsound. Even procedures for solving equations may not be able to take hold. *The Truth* is a routine designed to help students practice their understanding of the equal sign in any grade and with a wide variety of operations and number types.

Why It Matters

This routine helps students:

- experience problems that are not routine word or story problems (MP1);

- reason about how numbers are related (MP2);
- consider how operations affect values (MP2);

 All tasks can be downloaded for your use at **resources.corwin.com/ jumpstartroutines/elementary**

- strengthen their understanding of equations as tools for solving problems (MP5);
- justify their conclusions (MP3);

- improve precision (MP6); and
- identify patterns and structure within equations to draw conclusions without calculating (MP7).

What They Should Understand First

Obviously, students should understand the meaning of the equal sign to some extent before working with the routine. Students do not necessarily need to master the concept in order to work with the routine, as it is intended to support this pursuit. The routine itself should not be an introduction to new ideas about the values on either side of an equation. For example, students who have worked with sums and differences only appearing on the right side of the equal sign are not good candidates to work with operations on both sides of the equation without new instruction. It is also noteworthy that fact recall is not a requirement for working with this routine. You can support students with fact charts, number charts, and other tools to help them work with the computations in the routine as needed.

What to Do

1. Create equations to present to students. Consider creating equations that are related in some way so that students can apply ideas about one equation to another. The equations presented in the featured example show what this might look like as 16 is a value presented in each equation.

2. Consider providing tools to support student thinking. You might use 10 frames to help model the equations. Number charts, number lines, or even calculators can be used to support computation.

3. Present one equation to students.

4. Have students determine if the equation is true or false and share their thinking with a partner.

5. Bring the class together to discuss how students determined if the equation is true. Questions to ask might include:
   » How did you determine if the equation was true?
   » Was there something you knew that told you it had to be true or false?
   » Was there something about the equation that surprised you when you learned it was true or false?

6. Pose a second equation. Have students determine if the equation is true or false and turn to a partner to share their thinking.

7. Have a class discussion about the second equation. Questions to ask during the discussion include:
   » How did you determine if this (second) equation was true?
   » Did you have to do the computation to determine if it was true?
   » What other math facts do you know that helped you think about this equation?
   » How does your model (if students use a tool) connect to the equation?
   » How is the second equation related to the first equation?

8. Repeat the process for the next one or two equations. Time may restrict the number of equations you may use on a given day. You can present third and fourth equations on the following day with solutions to the first two also in place. Or you might use those equations as homework adding a prompt like *show how you know* so that students can again practice their reasoning.

9. Honor and explore both accurate and flawed thinking.

Anticipated Strategies for This Example

TRUE or FALSE	
A. $10 + 6 = 16$	B. $16 = 8 + 7$
C. $9 + 7 = 16$	D. $16 = 11 + 5$

$10 + 6 = 16$ is a good equation to begin with in this version of *The Truth*. Students are likely to determine if it is true with some ease. Some will quote a plus-10 fact. Others are able to count on 6 using tools or simply counting in their heads. Still others will note that there is one 10 added to six ones so the sum is one 10 and six ones or 16. Students may then use that information to make sense of other equations. For example, if they know that Equation A is true then Equation C is also true because one can be given from 10 to 6 to make the $9 + 7$ in Equation C. Students might not always use the relationships between equations. They might see equations as isolated *things*. In other cases, students might simply know a sum, difference, or other result so that little thought is given to the truth of the equation presented. Equation B might be one of those possibilities. Students who know that $8 + 8 = 16$ will recognize that $8 + 7$ can't equal 16. Even so, as sums and differences are moved to the left side of an equation students might no longer make use of facts that they know.

THE TRUTH—ADDITIONAL EXAMPLES

A. Students must work with sums and differences that are on both sides of the equal sign. Once students understand this, you can help them advance to more complicated ideas about equations. The first place to move them might be to use different operations in the same routine. As you might notice, the featured routine has sums on both sides of the equation but all equations use addition. Example A uses both addition and subtraction. You can then levy connections between operations. For example, Equations C and D are related though it might not appear so at first. Upon closer examintation and a bit of reasoning, students might conclude that D is true because 10 is added to both the minuend and the subtrahend so that the difference remains unchanged.

A. TRUE or FALSE	
A. $15 = 8 + 8$	B. $25 - 18 = 8$
C. $17 - 8 = 9$	D. $9 = 27 - 18$

B. You can use *The Truth* for practice with other emerging skills and concepts, which also helps fortify student understanding of the equal sign. Example B shows how *The Truth* can make use of both multi-digit numbers and mixed operations. As the complexity of numbers change in later grades, you might first rely on the same operation (as shown in the featured example). In time, you can mix other operations as in Examples A and B. As students work with multi-digit numbers within these equations, it is important to help them consider *if* they need to compute to prove if the equation is true or false. In some cases, they will need to find the exact result. In others, like Equation B they can reason. Here, neither addend is 200 so the sum can't be 400, let alone 488.

B	TRUE or FALSE	
A. $53 = 25 + 28$		B. $488 = 181 + 207$
C. $175 = 205 - 40$		D. $102 = 501 - 399$

C. First graders and early second graders might not be ready to work with two- or three-digit addends. But, there are other important concepts to develop with them which will provide appropriate challenge. One way to modify the challenge is to place more than two addends on either side of the equation. Another, as shown in Example C, is to offer different operations on either side of the equation.

C	TRUE or FALSE	
A. $9 + 6 = 8 + 5$		B. $17 - 7 - 3 = 3 + 7$
C. $4 + 7 = 3 + 7 + 1$		D. $3 + 3 = 11 - 5$

D. As students begin to learn about multiplication and division, they might revert to thinking that the right side of an equation is *the answer*, which in these cases is the product or quotient. You can modify *The Truth* to accommodate these operations. Example D might not be the best place to begin with students. Instead, it is provided to help you think about the many ways that you can present multiplication and division. In time, you can pose multiplication and division equations in the same occurrence of the routine (Equations A, B, and C). Giving equations with multiplication on both sides of the equation is also a possibility (Equation D). Advanced challenges might show addition on one side of the equation and multiplication or division on the other side.

D	TRUE or FALSE	
A. $7 \times 5 = 75$		B. $8 = 32 \div 4$
C. $10 = 4 \div 4$		D. $4 \times 3 = 2 \times 6$

THE TRUTH VARIATION—COMPUTATION

Like any concept in elementary mathematics, fundamental ideas are first introduced in kindergarten. This is true for comparison of number, addition, and subtraction. It is also true for the meaning of the equal sign. In most cases, kindergarten students do not have to explain the meaning of the equal sign. But, they can rationalize that one thing is the same as the other.

E. Example E might be used with kindergarteners during the second half of the year, if not sooner. They aren't asked if the two things are *equal*. Instead, they determine if one is the same as the other. However, it would not be surprising for a handful of students to use equal and to describe it accurately without formal instruction. Nonetheless, 10 frame cards are a good place to start so that *same as* can be established. Teachers should record digits during discussion to connect symbolic representations to visual representations. It is optional to provide students with 10 frames that they can manipulate during the routine. They might be used at first before removing them for later experiences.

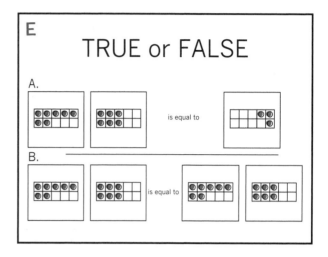

F. As noted throughout this book, students of all ages need opportunities to work with diverse representations of number. The same is true when using *The Truth* with kindergarteners. Example F shows domino cards.

Like Example E, students determine if one domino is the same as another. Interesting conversation is likely to take place. In both cases, students might think they are the same because any two have 6 pips on one side. When this happens, highlight how they are different and shift focus to the number of pips in total on each domino. Students may also rely visually on the difference to determine if they are the same as they can see one has more pips than the other. When this occurs, your conversation should support the difference and connect it to symbolic representations (numbers). Also note that domino cards do not need to be downloaded and printed. Real dominoes could easily be projected as well.

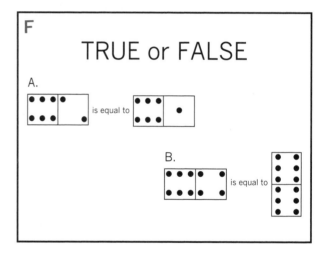

online resources — These cards can be downloaded for your use at resources.corwin.com/jumpstartroutines/elementary

THE TRUTH VARIATION—FRACTIONS AND DECIMALS

The Truth is just one more routine that can build fraction and decimal sense. Working with these numbers can be difficult for students. Without being careful, equations with fractions and decimals might consistently have the sum or difference positioned on the right of the equal sign.

G. Example G shows how you can use fractions in the routine. Of course, you might use like denominators first before unlike denominators. In some grades, unlike denominators shouldn't be considered at all. You might also help students reason about the two sides of the equations before attempting to find exact results. With this reasoning, students might determine that one side of the equation is more than one and the other is less than one so then the equation must not be true. For example, in Equation B $\frac{12}{6} - \frac{4}{6}$ is more than one and $\frac{1}{3} + \frac{1}{3}$ is less than one so that equation cannot be true. No calculation is needed to determine if it is.

Example G lifts up another idea that you might use in the routine. C and D present students with comparisons. This is not within the requirements of elementary mathematics standards. However, it doesn't mean that students can't think or reason about it. After all, determining if two sides of an equation are equal is not much different than determining if one thing is greater than another.

G

TRUE or FALSE

A.
$$\frac{3}{4} + \frac{3}{4} = \frac{5}{4} + \frac{1}{4}$$

B.
$$\frac{12}{6} - \frac{4}{6} = \frac{1}{3} + \frac{1}{3}$$

C.
$$\frac{7}{3} > \frac{5}{4} + \frac{1}{4}$$

D.
$$\frac{8}{4} + \frac{3}{2} + \frac{1}{2} > 3$$

H. Example H uses decimals within the routine. This example is best reserved for late fifth grade. Even then, students should first work with *friendly decimals*, which are included in Equations A, C, and D. The decimals in Equation B (0.43 and 0.03) are not as friendly but still relatively easy to think about, especially in the context of this equation. Equations with decimals should be carefully created so that students have just as many opportunities to think as they have to compute. Equation A is an example of this. Some students will be tempted to *line up the decimals* to add. But, others might reason that 4 + 7 = 11 and 4 + 7.5 = 11.5 so then 4.5 + 7.5 cannot equal 11.5.

H

TRUE or FALSE

A.	B.
4.5 + 7.5 = 11.5	17.43 = 3.03 + 14.40

C.	D.
35 − 7.75 = 28.25	16 = 20.5 − 4 − 0.5

PART 3

WHERE TO GO NEXT

You are now armed with understanding why routines matter and how they develop number sense and reasoning. You hopefully see how they can engage your students. You have examined a host of examples and modifications ready to implement in your classroom. So, where do you go next?

MAKE A PLAN

Using routines in your mathematics classrooms might be considerably different than what has been done previously. To be successful, you need to craft a plan that addresses fundamental considerations. First, identify the mathematics concepts and content you want to focus on with your students. Next, determine which routines you think will work best. Think about a rotation of routines and whether you will change routines out daily or if you will work with one routine for a few days before moving to the next. Set goals for your work.

Identify Content for Routines

Routines are not intended as first instruction or reteaching of mathematics concepts. They should be opportunities for students to practice and apply the skills and concepts they have already attained. Routines should be engagement opportunities for reasoning and discussion. The skills, concepts, or numbers that you select should be relative to where your students are. It is okay that some classrooms will need to work with counting principles or estimation with smaller numbers. The intent is to advance all students' reasoning and mental mathematics abilities. You should also keep in mind that all of the routines have the flexibility to accommodate any of the skills, concepts, or numbers that you select.

Identify Routines

It's likely that every teacher has a preference for certain representations, strategies, or techniques in general. The same can probably be said about the preference of routines. There is a collection of routines presented here. Some may be simply more appealing than others. The intent is to provide options rather than a sequence of routines to *cover* or *complete*.

Your goal should be to choose a few routines that you want to master first. You might make your selection based on students' interests. You might choose a routine like *Picture It* because you want to improve your students' general sense of number and magnitude. You might choose it because each and every student can engage with the images. You might like *Math Yapper* because it has a high-engagement factor. You might select it because you need to further develop your students' use of vocabulary. You might select *Where's the Point?* and *Is This the End?* because you want to develop your students' understanding of number relationships and number lines, respectively.

Determine the Rotation

Doing the same routine each day will become mundane quite quickly. Even if it doesn't, you might find that your students continuously employ the same types of reasoning or arguments. To avoid this, it is important to rotate the routines to keep engagement and thinking fresh. You might first work for a week or so with a certain routine such as *The Count.* Then, you might rotate to *How Can You Make It?* for a week or so. You might then follow with *About or Between* and *More or Less* in a similar manner. After the fourth routine, you might circle back to your first routine, *The Count.* You could rotate through the four routines again. In doing this, you become more comfortable with each routine on the first pass so that you are better prepared to implement them all on the second pass. After a second or third rotation, you might begin to change out each routine for something new.

It's important to realize that you don't have to dedicate a specific number of days or class periods to a routine before rotating to another. The time spent with two different routines may not be equivalent. You can plan the amount of time you spend with a routine based on students' needs, engagement, interest, and excitement for it. However, even if you spend a few extra days with a certain routine, you should plan to move on from it so that it doesn't become stale. You should be mindful of those routines that students truly enjoy and plan to come back to them throughout the year.

Give It Time

It's unlikely that many of your students have had many opportunities to work with activities not directly related to the concepts they are learning. Others have likely had few opportunities to engage in thinking and reasoning activities grounded in number sense and mental mathematics. That number of students probably diminishes further when you factor in opportunities for discussion and justification of reasoning and number sense. Most, if not all, of your students will at some point have started a mathematics lesson that features homework review and low-level warmup. This may be uncharted waters for them.

This may be unchartered waters for you, too. Many teachers are trained to plan an obligatory warm-up. They are led to believe that going over homework is a mathematics constitutional right. They have not or could not think about different ways to launch a class. Your first routine, or two, may flop because of you and your students' unfamiliarity. That is fine. It should be expected. Be patient. The best course of action is to plan and implement a routine for a few days and then adjust, but not eliminate.

Set Goals

You can offset the challenges with goals, but your goals should be reasonable. At first, you might set the goal of doing a routine three times a week or mastering a specific routine over the course of two weeks. You might set a goal to use three different routines in the course of a month or five different routines in a marking period.

You can think about setting goals for students as well. You might want to develop their use of vocabulary. You might want them to demonstrate their ability to justify their thinking or to critique the reasoning of others. You might set goals that are content specific. You can measure those goals in all sorts of ways. One way might be to revisit a routine from early in the year with the exact same numbers or concepts later in the year and compare student performance. In other situations, it might make sense to measure growing student proficiency on a brief written assessment that measures reasoning, fluency, or number sense. You might also measure student behaviors, interactions, communication skills, and confidence.

ADJUST TO THEIR ADJUSTMENTS

You naturally respond to student thinking and reasoning. You ask questions to challenge student ideas. You push back on students' strategies. You ask them to clarify. You'll need to leverage those same teacher moves during routines. You'll also need to keep in mind that as students work with routines, they'll begin to adjust their reasoning. They may begin to favor specific strategies or approaches. When they do, you'll need to respond by changing the numbers, skills, and concepts that you feature. For example, in a routine such as *The Missing* students might show proficiency and comfort with ideas of one more and 10 more. When this happens, you can adjust given numbers so that students have to make use of two more, one less, 10 less, and so on. In *Is This the End?*, you might first challenge students with number lines that have a known midpoint but unknown endpoints. As they adapt to the routine, you can then start to move the known location places such as a quarter point.

FURTHER MODIFY ROUTINES

Each of the routines here are creations or adaptations of activities used in real classrooms. They have served real students well. There are directions and procedures for implementing them; but those directions are not set in stone. In fact, many of the routines presented are variations of the first offerings. There are ideas for modifying presented throughout, but more can be changed. You should feel free to change the direction of how you present routines. Adjust them to make them their own.

DESIGN YOUR OWN ROUTINES

These routines are all built on the notions of reasoning and number sense. They all feature opportunities for students to discuss and defend their reasoning. You can modify almost any activity to become a routine. As you become more comfortable with routines, you can begin to develop your own based on games and activities you use during instruction. You can look for routines online. You might even investigate the routines that are available for middle school to consider you might modify and incorporate them in your own instruction.

Students might even take the next step and create their own examples from the various routines. Bloom's revised taxonomy places create at the very top of the triangle.

Bloom's Taxonomy

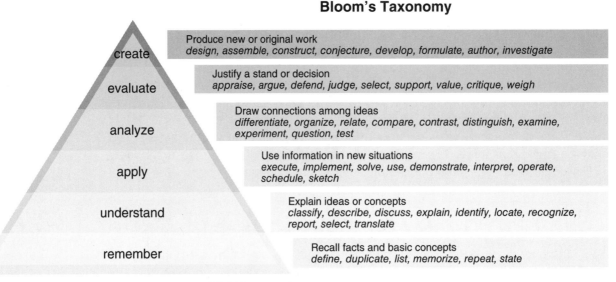

Bloom's Taxonomy. Created by @cirtlmooc http://hiscience.pbworks.com/t/1467974486/Bloomtaxonomy.jpg; Creative commons Attribution 2.0 Generic (CC BY 2.0) https://creativecommons.org/licenses/by-sa/2.0/

When students produce new or original work, they are working at the highest cognitive process dimension.

WORK COLLABORATIVELY AND SHARE THE LOAD

Sometimes your students' creative thinking will inspire new possibilities or new routines. Keep in mind that your colleagues are also an excellent creative source for generating examples. When teachers plan together, they learn about others' perspectives, experiences, and mathematical insights. They learn about how others think and reason about numbers and computation. The exchange of ideas with your colleagues can help you reinforce and grow your own ideas. It helps you prepare. It helps you facilitate student reasoning through discussion.

Leveraging insights from other teachers and students is also a great way to share the workload. For example, four teachers on a team could each create four sets of prompts for a routine. If those four teachers share their four, each teacher would have a routine planned for 16 days, or a little more than three weeks. Each of those teachers could also have students create examples of their routine. If so, they could select four student examples and rotate them as well. In doing so, a teacher who created four examples could wind up with 32 days ready to go.

USE JUMP-START ROUTINES FOR PROFESSIONAL LEARNING OR PLCS

Routines are the perfect focus for professional learning or a professional learning community (PLC). In fact, many of the routines offered in this book are the result of ongoing collaborative conversations, dabbling, and reflection. In a PLC about routines, you might first learn about what routines are, why they matter, and the instructional challenges they intend to solve. You and your colleagues can then begin to learn about specific routines, try them out, and share your experiences. The steps below are a helpful framework for investigating and learning about routines in a PLC.

1. Learn About the Routine: Colleagues select a routine that they all want to focus on. They read about it and discuss what it might look like or how it might be adjusted for their students.

2. Identify Content for the Routine: Colleagues discuss what types of mathematics content, numbers, number relationships, or operations they would feature in the routine and why.

3. Create Examples: Colleagues select or create examples of the routine for use with their students. One way to do this is to make use of collaborative software, such as Google slides, in which each teacher can craft some examples of the routine they intend to use with their students. Making use of a collaboration tool allows those teachers to have a record of their work for future use and share examples between them. Sharing examples also helps lessen the workload.

4. Predict What Might Happen: After making examples of the routine to use with students, colleagues anticipate what their students will do. They might share the strategies that students will use, the misconceptions they might show, or the questions that the teachers themselves might ask.

5. Do Them: Members of the PLC do the routines with their students.

6. Reflect: Individuals jot down notes or capture reflections about the routine. Those reflections are brought to the next meeting in which colleagues share their experiences and consider what went well and what they might do differently in the future.

These six steps are then started again with a new routine. There are no rules as to how this has to proceed. There is logic exploring the same routines with your colleagues. However, the PLC can play out just as well if you and they select your own routines to use.

The work of the PLC might be strengthened through peer observation and feedback. To do this, you simply visit one another and look for how routines are being implemented. Then, you give and receive feedback from your colleagues about how things went. Peer observations can be supported with a *look for* tool. It's quite possible that colleagues don't have the time to visit each other during the day. Another option might be for you to make a video of your routine for others to view and offer feedback.

Look For It

There are all sorts of things one might look for when visiting a colleague doing a routine. Some of those ideas are below. The list is not exhaustive. You could also consider this as a list of things to think about before you begin to work with your routines.

The classroom environment is conducive to a routine.

- Student proximity to the teacher is appropriate.
- Student arrangement promotes discussion between students and as a class.
- Respectful behaviors are established.
- Students are comfortable sharing ideas.

The routine is appropriate.

- The concepts have been taught (though not necessarily mastered).
- The selected numbers are appropriate.
- The routine focuses on reasoning and sense making.

Multiple solutions/rationales are investigated/discussed.

- Multiple answers are solicited first.
- Strategies are recorded and/or discussed.
- Thinking is recorded accurately.
- More than one solution pathway is investigated.

Communication is prevalent.

- Students share their reasoning.
- Students listen and react to the reasoning of others.
- Teachers react to student reasoning by asking questions.

Discussion promotes reasoning.

- More than one perspective is featured.
- Teachers question overly complicated or highly-inefficient strategies.

Teachers question if representations are warranted or practical.

 You can find this checklist/tool at **resources.corwin.com/jumpstartroutines/elementary**

JUMP-START MATHEMATICS ENGAGEMENT, NUMBER SENSE, AND REASONING

Starting each mathematics class with a routine is an opportunity to jump-start engagement, number sense, and reasoning. These routines are quality tasks for working with a wide range of skills and concepts. They are opportunities for promoting engagement through novel prompts, interesting situations, and discussion. They are opportunities to play with numbers. They are a chance for us to do something about the rhetorical "They just don't have number sense" or "They just don't know how to think."

APPENDIX

ROUTINE	NUMBER SENSE PURPOSE	STANDARDS FOR MATHEMATICAL PRACTICE							
		MP1	MP2	MP3	MP4	MP5	MP6	MP7	MP8
Math Yapper	Communicating about math	X		X			X		
The Count	Counting and skip-counting		X	X				X	
The Missing	Counting and skip-counting	X	X	X		X		X	X
Big or Small	Magnitude		X	X					
Picture It	Magnitude and estimation	X	X	X	X				
Show It 3	Representing numbers	X	X	X	X	X		X	
How Can You Make It?	Decomposition		X	X			X	X	X
The Mighty Ten	Combinations of tens, hundreds, or thousands		X	X		X	X		X
Make It Friendly	Compatible numbers		X	X		X	X	X	
Mystery Number	Number concepts and relationships	X	X	X				X	
Number Bio	Number concepts and relationships	X	X	X				X	
Condition	Flexible thinking		X	X			X		
Where's the Point?	Number line relationships	X	X	X	X				
Is This the End?	Number line relationships	X	X	X	X				X
About or Between	Estimating results		X	X			X		
More or Less	Estimating results		X	X		X	X		
This or That?	Estimating and comparing	X	X	X			X	X	X
Finding One and All	Efficient computation	X	X	X				X	X
Another Way to Say It	Efficient computation		X	X		X	X	X	X
The Truth	Meaning of the equal sign	X	X	X		X	X	X	

REFERENCES

Arizona Department of Education. (2018). *Fluency of mathematics: Kindergarten – Algebra 2*. Retrieved from https://cms.azed.gov/home/GetDocumentFile?id=591b82103217e1221c5e8c92

Bay-Williams, J., & Fletcher, G. (2017). A Bottom-Up Hundred Chart? *Teaching Children Mathematics, 24*, 3.

Boaler, J. (2015). *Mathematical mindsets: Unleashing students' potential through creative math, inspiring messages, and innovative teaching*. San Francisco, CA: Jossey-Bass.

Boaler, J. (2015, May 7). Memorizers are the lowest achievers and other Common Core math surprises. Retrieved from http://hechingerreport.org/memorizers-are-the-lowest-achievers-and-other-common-core-math-surprises/

Cooper, H. (2006, September 23). Does homework improve academic achievement? Retrieved from https://today.duke.edu/2006/09/homework_oped.html

Dweck, C. (2006). *Mindset: The new psychology of success*. New York, NY: Penguin Random House.

Fennell, F., & Landis, T. E. (1994). Number sense and operation sense. In C. A. Thornton & N. S. Bley (Eds.), *Windows of opportunity: Mathematics for students with special needs* (pp. 187–203). Reston, VA: National Council of Teachers of Mathematics.

Gelman, R., & Gallistel, C. R. (1978). *The child's understanding of number*. Cambridge, MA: Harvard University Press.

Gladwell, M. (2008). *Outliers: The story of success*. New York, NY: Little, Brown and Company.

Grouws, D. A., Tarr, J. E., Sears, R., & Ross, D. J. (2010). *Mathematics teachers' use of instructional time and relationships to textbook content organization and class period format*. Paper presented at the Hawaii International Conference on Education, Honolulu, Hawaii.

Krasa, N., & Shunkwiler, S. (2009). *Number sense and number nonsense: Understanding the challenges of learning math*. Grand Rapids, MI: Paul H. Brookes Publishing Company.

Lesh, R., Post, T., & Behr, M. (1987). Representations and translations among representations in mathematics learning and problem solving. In C. Janvier (Ed.), *Problems of representation in the teaching and learning of mathematics* (pp. 33–40). Hillsdale, NJ: Erlbaum.

National Council of Teachers of Mathematics. (1989). *Curriculum and evaluation standards for school mathematics*. Reston, VA: Author.

National Council of Teachers of Mathematics. (2000). *Principles and standards for school mathematics*. Reston, VA: Author.

National Council of Teachers of Mathematics. (2014). *Principles to actions: Ensuring mathematical success for all*. Reston, VA: Author.

National Governors Association Center for Best Practices, Council of Chief State School Officers. (2010). *Common core state standards, mathematics*. Washington, DC: Author.

National Research Council. (2001). *Adding it up: Helping children learn mathematics* J. Kilpatrick, J. Swafford, & B. Findell (Eds.). Washington, DC: National Academies Press.

O'Connell, S., & SanGiovanni, J. (2013). *Putting practice into action: Implementing the common core standards for mathematical practice*. Portsmouth, NH: Heinemann.

Otten, S., Herbel-Eisenmann, B. A., & Cirillo, M. (2012). Going over homework in mathematics classrooms: An unexamined activity. Retrieved from http://www.tcrecord.org/Content.asp?contentid=16851

Parrish, S. (2010). *Number Talks, Math Solutions*. Boston, MA: Houghton Mifflin Harcourt Publishing.

Skemp, R. R. (2006). Relational understanding and instrumental understanding. *Mathematics Teaching in the Middle School, 12*, 88–95.

Smith, M. S., & Stein, M. K. (2018). *5 practices for orchestrating productive mathematics discussions* (2nd ed.). Reston, VA: National Council of Teachers of Mathematics.

Sousa, D. (2007). *How the brain learns mathematics*. Thousand Oaks, CA: Corwin.

Van de Walle, J. A., Karp, K. S., & Bay-Williams, J. M. (2019). *Elementary and middle school mathematics: Teaching developmentally* (10th ed.). New York, NY: Pearson.

Wyborney, S. (2018). *20 Days of Number Sense & Rich Math Talk (K-12)*. Retrieved from www.stevewyborney.com

NOTES

NOTES

NOTES

NOTES

NOTES

NOTES

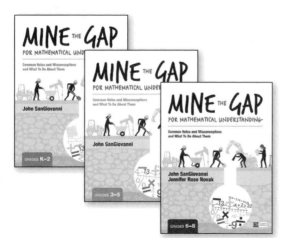

ALL students should have the opportunity to be successful in mathematics!

Trusted experts in mathematics education offer clear and practical guidance to help students move from surface to deep mathematical understanding, from procedural to conceptual learning, and from rote memorization to true comprehension. Through books, videos, consulting, and online tools, we offer a truly blended learning experience that helps you demystify mathematics for students.

Move the needle on math instruction with these 5 assessment techniques

Francis (Skip) Fennell, Beth McCord Kobett, and Jonathan A. Wray

Grades K–8

Your blueprint to planning math lessons that lead to achievement for all learners

Beth McCord Kobett, Ruth Harbin Miles, and Lois A. Williams

Grades K–2
Grades 3–5
Grades 6–8

New Series Based on the Bestselling *Visible Learning for Mathematics*

Maximize student achievement in mathematics with Visible Learning

John Almarode, Douglas Fisher, Joseph Assof, Sara Delano Moore, Kateri Thunder, John Hattie, and Nancy Frey

Research tells us which mathematical teaching practices can be effective. Now we know which are the most effective, when they're the most effective, and how they can be used to foster student-centered, visible learning. The suite of *Visible Learning for Mathematics* resources helps you to

- plan lessons with clear learning intentions and success criteria,
- which teaching strategies to use *when*, based on learning goals and feedback, and
- foster metacognition so that students can own their learning journeys.

Find strategies and tools to help you have the greatest impact on your students' learning, all informed by the world's largest educational research database.

Discover Visible Learning research, tools, and more at **corwin.com/VLforMath**

CORWIN
A SAGE Publishing Company

Helping educators make the greatest impact

CORWIN HAS ONE MISSION: to enhance education through intentional professional learning.

We build long-term relationships with our authors, educators, clients, and associations who partner with us to develop and continuously improve the best evidence-based practices that establish and support lifelong learning.